Ned Miner and His Pioneering Forebears

Edward Griffith Miner, 1863–1955

Ned Miner and His Pioneering Forebears

Edward Miner Lamont

MELIORA PRESS

An imprint of the University of Rochester Press

First published 2010

Meliora Press is an imprint of the
University of Rochester Press
668 Mt. Hope Avenue, Rochester, NY 14620, USA
www.urpress.com
and Boydell & Brewer Limited
PO Box 9, Woodbridge, Suffolk IP12 3DF, UK
www.boydellandbrewer.com

ISBN-13: 978-1-58046-384-3

Library of Congress Cataloging-in-Publication Data

Lamont, Edward M., 1926–
    Ned Miner and his pioneering forebears / Edward Miner Lamont.
      p. cm.
    Includes bibliographical references.
    ISBN 978-1-58046-384-3 (hardcover : alk. paper) 1. Miner, Edward Griffith, 1863–1955. 2. Businessmen—United States—Biography. 3. United States—Social conditions—19th century. 4. United States—Social conditions—20th century. I. Title.
    HC102.5.M5L36 2010
    338.7'6602832092—dc22
    [B]

                                                                2010042671

This publication is printed on acid-free paper.
Printed in the United States of America.

To all the Miners,
past and present

Contents

Introduction   1

I.   The Stonington Miners   3
II.   Go West, Young Man   8
III.   Abraham Lincoln Comes to Winchester   12
IV.   The Country Doctor   17
V.   Ned Miner Comes to Rochester   32
VI.   Rochester's Remarkable Citizen   39
VII.   The Miners of Argyle Street   49

Acknowledgments   57

Sources   59

Introduction

In the spring of 2009, Ranlet Miner and I, along with our wives, Beth and Camille, spent a few days in Rochester, New York, the longtime home of Ranny's and my grandparents, Edward Griffith Miner and Helen Ranlet Miner. They had lived in Rochester for over sixty years before Grandfather died in 1955 and Grandmother in 1964. Ranny had grown up in Rochester, and I had visited my grandparents there many times, including our family's biannual Christmas get-together with our Miner relatives. Their comfortable old home was also a welcome refuge for me in 1945 when I was in the navy, stationed at the Sampson Naval Training Base in Geneva, New York.

Ranny and I were invited by officials of the University of Rochester Medical School to tour the school and receive a briefing concerning the Edward G. Miner Library of the Medical School. Along with our informative meetings at the University, the trip was, for me, a sentimental journey that stirred old memories as we stopped by places where my Miner grandparents had lived their lives.

We first viewed their graves in the lovely old Mount Hope Cemetery with its grassy knolls and shady paths, and then drove down East Avenue past St. Paul's Church. Both our parents had been married in the church where E. G. Miner had served on the vestry for many years. Later we knocked on the door of 2 Argyle Street, the massive red brick mansion that had been our grandparents' home. It looked the same as ever—big, solid, and undistinguished. The owner greeted us warmly and showed us about. The big house had been divided into eight single-bedroom apartments, designed quite tastefully around the central staircase that we remembered well. Some of the tenants were teachers or professors at the University of Rochester, the landlady told us proudly. This would have pleased Grandfather, who had been Chairman of the Board of Trustees of the university, and had actively supported its development over many years.

Our Rochester visits and talks reminded me again that E. G. Miner had not only led the growth of a successful and important manufacturing company in Rochester; he had also become a highly respected and admired community leader in his hometown. And Ned Miner, as he was known to his friends, was by no means the first Miner in America to serve his community actively. Engaging in public service was a common trait that went back generations in the family.

A few weeks later, Camille and I visited the Abraham Lincoln Presidential Museum in Springfield, Illinois, with some friends who were Lincoln fans like ourselves. Lincoln had lived in Springfield for twenty-five years, where he practiced law and served as a representative in the state's General Assembly, before he became President. The state-of-the-art museum, the Lincoln Library, and Lincoln's home and tomb were all fascinating places for Lincoln buffs to visit.

But I also had a personal interest in visiting the region. My great-great grandfather Edward G. Miner, after whom Grandfather was named, left Vermont in 1832 to settle in the small frontier hamlet of Winchester, Illinois, some fifty miles west of Springfield. In Winchester, which was our next stop, Miner had come to know Abraham Lincoln before he became President, as well as Stephen A. Douglas. Miner's son, my great grandfather, Dr. James Miner, also lived in Winchester, as did Grandfather before he left for Rochester in 1883, when he was nineteen years old.

Winchester is now a small, sleepy town of about seventeen hundred residents in the flat farm country of western Illinois. It boasts a handsome statue of Stephen A. Douglas at the center of the town square near the county court house. The local historian, an elderly attorney, directed us to the old E. G. Miner farm home, a sturdy, red brick house occupied by a local family who were not at home when we stopped by. Our historian friend noted the nineteenth-century Miners' civic contributions to Winchester. But, sadly, there were no longer any Miners left in those parts for us to meet.

Nowadays, my daughter, Camille Burlingham, lives in Stonington, Connecticut, where the first of my Miner forebears to immigrate to the New World, Thomas Minor (as his family styled their name), settled in 1653. An imposing granite monument in the old town cemetery honors him and three other founding settlers of the town, which was a rugged frontier settlement in those days. After my visits to Winchester and Stonington, I decided that the time had come to pull together the pieces of the story of my Miner forebears, from pioneer to industrialist, a story that, in one sense, illustrates the growth of America as it came of age.

I. The Stonington Miners

Thomas Minor was born in 1608 in the little Norman English village of Chew Magna, tucked away in the rolling Mendits hills of Somerset County, England, where his father, Clement Miner, and earlier Miner families had lived for over a century. The family probably took its name from their occupation, as lead mining had taken place in that hilly region since Roman times. Thomas, the youngest of Clement Miner's eight children, chose to spell his name as some in previous generations had done. Boldly deciding to cast his lot with the venturesome Puritan settlers in the fledgling Massachusetts Bay colony in New England, Minor embarked from Gravesend with forty fellow emigrants and six fishermen aboard the ship *Lyon's Whelp* on April 25, 1629. The *Lyon's Whelp* reached Salem, Massachusetts, in mid-July after a rough and stormy voyage of almost three months. After the Pilgrims founded the first New England colony, the Plymouth Plantation, in 1620, a company of Cape Ann fishermen started a small outpost in Salem, which was assumed by the Massachusetts Bay Company in 1626.

After an outbreak of typhoid fever in Salem, Minor moved quickly on to the settlement of Watertown and, after a brief stay there, he settled in nearby Charlestown. A loyal member of the Puritan movement, Minor became a founder of the new Congregational Church built in that settlement. In 1634 he wed Grace Palmer, the daughter of Walter Palmer of Charlestown. After a couple of years the Minors moved to nearby Hingham and started raising a family. But Thomas was restless, and ready to embark on a promising new venture when the opportunity arose.

In 1645, under a commission from the General Court of Massachusetts to start a plantation in the Pequot Colony in Connecticut, Minor joined John Winthrop Jr.'s group of Massachusetts Puritans in establishing the new settlement, later known as New London. Some months later, Grace and their five sons, all born over the last decade, made the move to New London to join Thomas. Another son, Manassah, was the first male child born in New London. There the Miners also had two daughters, who both died in childhood.

John Winthrop Jr. was the son of the forceful Puritan leader and governor of Massachusetts Bay Colony. The colony's leaders soon recognized Minor as a person of sound judgment and initiative. In 1649 he was appointed sergeant of the New London Train Band (the local militia) and assistant magistrate for the town. In 1650 and 1651 he represented New London as a deputy to sessions of the Connecticut General Court in Hartford, the colonial seat of government.

In 1653 Thomas Minor was on the move again. He sold his New London property and moved his family to settle in a new area in Connecticut, present-day Stonington, then known as Southerton. Facing the ocean and featuring wide salt marshes, snug harbors, bays, and coves, the little settlement would become an active port in the future. There the Minors had another son, Samuel, born in 1653; their last child, Hannah, was born in 1655. Minor bought his prime property, a 252-acre tract in the new settlement, from his friend Carey Latham, and he built his home at Latham's Neck on Quiambaug Cove. Thomas Minor, William Chesebrough (a member of the first family to settle in the area), Thomas Stanton (who had built a trading post in 1650), and Minor's father-in-law, Walter Palmer, were the first settlers and founders of the new town. Today there is a granite monument dedicated to them in the Wequetequock Cemetery.

After he moved to Stonington, Thomas started keeping a diary, mainly a laconic day-to-day account of his farm operations and life in the little frontier settlement. In the mid-seventeenth century the region was still a wilderness area where Pequot and Narragansett Indians lived and wolves and bears attacked the Minor livestock. He put his "long gun" to good use in protecting his properties from wild animals, and in the Indian wars of 1675 and 1676. The Minor farm grew into a large operation. It produced a variety of vegetables, flax, hemp, wheat, and oats, and kept sheep, goats, hogs, oxen, and cattle. Minor himself put a great deal of hard physical labor into building a home for his large family, clearing the woodlands for farming, building stone walls to mark his property's boundaries, plowing and cultivating his fields, creating a fruit orchard, tending his livestock, and planting his gardens.

Fortunately, Thomas remained strong and fit until late in life. To assist him as he grew older, he had his seven able-bodied sons and his daughter, Hannah. He also employed a local man and from time to time hired Pequot Indians to help out. The Minor farm was largely self-sufficient in providing for the needs of the family. The few manufactured goods they bought from others were mainly paid for in kind with products from the farm—butter, beans, wheat, corn, cheese, and apple cider. Sometimes they also used wampum, the local Indian currency, to pay their debts. An August 1656 diary entry reads, "Bought wine and broke my schythe." There is no indication as to whether there was any connection between the two events.

Thomas soon became an active participant in the public administration of Stonington, as increasing numbers of families from Massachusetts arrived. A 1668 census recorded forty-three families living in the town. Minor was a Justice or Commissioner of the town throughout most of the 1660s and 1670s. From 1665 until 1689 he represented the town as a deputy at many of the sessions (in

Hartford) of the Connecticut General Court, the colony's legislative body, and served on several Court-appointed committees that dealt with land grant surveys, Indian relations, and setting the nearby boundary with Rhode Island. He also helped to organize the first church in Stonington.

His diary records that Governor John Winthrop Jr. was his guest from time to time, when presumably they discussed the affairs of Stonington and the colony. Winthrop was the popular governor of the Colony of Connecticut from 1659 until he died in 1676. Minor had some knowledge of the Algonquian language and was known for his good results in dealing with the local Indians. Several times Winthrop called on him to act as his envoy in delivering messages to the Narragansett and Monhegan tribes. In 1666 and 1667 Minor received 150 acres in colonial land grants in recognition of his public services.

In an April 1669 entry in his diary, Minor noted the various public offices that he held that year: "I was by the Town and this year chosen to be a selectman, the Town's Treasurer, the Town's Recorder, the brander of horses by the General Court, Recorded the Head Officer of the Train Band by the same Court—one of the four that have Charge of the militia of the whole County—and Chosen and sworn Commissioner and one to assist in keeping the County Court." Several years before, in 1665, Minor had been appointed Chief Military Officer of the Mystic Train Band. When King Philip's War broke out in 1675 between the English settlers and the Indians, who attacked many English communities in Connecticut, Minor served as a lieutenant in the militia. In December 1675 his troops joined militia companies from Connecticut and other New England colonies, about a thousand men in total, and attacked the large, fortified village of the Narragansett tribe near Kingston, Rhode Island. In the engagement, known as "The Great Swamp Fight," the Narragansetts fought fiercely to defend the fort housing their families. Finally, they ran out of gunpowder, and the militias stormed into the fort and set it and the wigwams inside on fire. The English dealt a crushing blow to the Narragansetts, killing more than three hundred of them, including women and children. The English casualties were heavy, too— around two hundred killed and wounded. The Connecticut militias suffered more casualties than those from any other colony—eighty dead and wounded from ranks totaling three hundred soldiers, reported their commanding officer. Thomas was fortunate to return home unscathed.

The Connecticut troops left the main force and marched back to Stonington on December 28. Thomas reported in his diary that he spent two months on military duty, before and after the battle. At age sixty-eight, he was surrounded by men less than half his age, including his sons Joseph and Manassah, who fought alongside their father as militia volunteers. Aside from the battle, the militias faced hard going through the bitter cold and heavy snows. After the war Minor received another colonial land grant as an award for his military service.

Thomas Minor is buried in the Wequetequock Cemetery in Stonington. The rough carving on the gravestone reads, "Here lyeth the body of Lieutenant

Thomas Minor, aged 83. Departed 1690." For the headstone, Thomas himself selected the flat piece of broken granite ledge, about the length of a man's body, from his farm. It is the oldest gravestone in the cemetery. His wife, Grace, died two months after her husband. The Minors left their land holdings to their children. Their youngest son, Samuel, received the prime Latham's Neck portion in recognition of his work in maintaining the farm and house when his parents were elderly. Another inscription regarding Minor on the four founders' monument in the cemetery states that he came to America on the ship *Arabella*, but later research has revealed that he came on the *Lyon's Whelp*. The inscription reads:

Lieut. Thomas Minor
Born in Chew Magna, Somerset County, England, April 23, 1608.
He was the first by the name of Minor to migrate to this country
coming on the ship *Arabella* which reached Salem Harbor June 14, 1630.
He married Grace, daughter of Walter Palmer, at Charlestown April 23, 1634.
He took up permanent abode at Quiambaug in 1653 or 1654
where he lived till his death October 23, 1690.
One of the founders of New London and Stonington.
Prominent in public office and organizer of the church.

Families were large in those days. Thomas Minor had fifty-six grandchildren, and the Miners proliferated in the Stonington area. Most of them reverted to the original English spelling of their surname, and "Miner" often appeared on the membership records of the Stonington town council and on rosters of local militias and the Continental Army during the Revolutionary War.

Four generations of E. G. Miner's forebears, the direct descendants of Thomas Minor, continued to live in Stonington and nearby towns throughout the 1700s. Thomas's fifth son, Joseph, born in 1644, was a Stonington physician as well as a farmer. Like his father, he was a volunteer member of the militia during King Philip's War and a deputy from Stonington to the General Court. Joseph first married Mary Avery of Togwonk, who died in 1708 after having born him three sons and five daughters. He then married the young widow Bridget Chesebrough, who gave birth to another daughter—probably not what Joseph was hoping for, given his need for more help on his farm as he grew older.

While farming was originally the main occupation in the area, in the eighteenth-century Stonington became known for ship building, fishing, whaling, and shipping in the triangle of trade between the West Indies and Europe. Over the next three generations, the Miners were reported to have become wealthy in the shipping business. They suffered substantial losses in the Revolutionary War, however. In 1775 the British frigate *Rose* bombarded Stonington, although the local militia prevented British troops from landing. During the war the town became a base for American privateers preying on British merchant shipping. Trade was disrupted by a British naval blockade of American ports. In 1781 the turncoat British general, Benedict Arnold, and strong British forces attacked and burned New London, destroying ships and warehouses. They seized Fort Griswold in Groton and slaughtered many of the captured American soldiers defending the fort.

Joseph's second son, Benjamin, born in 1676, married Mary Saxton and had five children. One was Clement, born in Stonington in 1706, who married Abigail Hempstead of New London and had ten children. His third son, Clement Jr., was born in 1738, and later married Mary Wheeler of Stonington and had six children. Clement Miner Jr. was commissioned as a second lieutenant in the Stonington company of the Connecticut militia on July 3, 1776, by Governor Jonathan Trumbell of Connecticut and helped defend Stonington and New London against the British attacks in the Revolutionary War.

Clement's son, Captain William Miner, born in Stonington in 1766, was a sea captain who sailed in the West Indies trade in his early years. Later he became part owner of a vessel, which was shipwrecked on its way from New London to the West Indies. After being picked up and brought back to his homeport by another ship, William moved his family to Vermont in 1798, where he went into farming. Edward Griffith Miner was the son of William and Prudence Potter Miner. He was born in Bridport, Vermont, on April 23, 1809, the youngest of six children.

Edward Griffith Miner Family Tree in America

Thomas Minor, b. 1608, d. 1690; m. Grace Palmer

Joseph Minor, b. 1644, d. 1712 (fifth son of Thomas); m. Mary Avery, Bridget Chesebrough

Benjamin Miner, b. 1676, d. 1711 (second son of Joseph); m. Mary Saxton

Clement Miner, b. 1706 (second son of Benjamin); m. Abigail Hempstead

Clement Miner Jr., b. 1738, d. 1787 (third son of Clement); m. Mary Wheeler

William Miner, b. 1766, d. 1813 (first son of Clement); m. Prudence Potter

Edward Griffith Miner, b. 1809, d. 1900 (fourth son of William); m. Sophronia Alden

Dr. James Miner, b. 1835, d. 1925 (first son of Edward); m. Eleanor Hawthorne Thomas

Edward Griffith Miner, b. 1863, d. 1955 (second son of James); m. Helen Branscombe Ranlet

II. Go West, Young Man

Edward's father, William, died when Edward was four years old. Times were hard for the Miner family; it was a difficult struggle to make ends meet. Even during his childhood Edward was forced to draw on his own resources. When he was fourteen he went to live with a cousin of his father in Milton, Vermont, where he worked in his uncle's woolen factory and learned the trade. At age nineteen he attended and taught at an academy in Jericho, Vermont. The next year he returned to Milton and took a job clerking in a dry goods store. He also acquired the skill of blacksmithing along the way, which would come in handy in his next venture.

The pioneering Miner spirit remained alive and well. In 1832 Edward was hired to drive a team of horses and a wagon with a party of people from Middlebury, Vermont, to Winchester, Illinois. Illinois had become a state in 1818, and the west central part of the state, where Winchester was located, was opening up for settlement. Miner's party left Middlebury on August 29 and reached Winchester forty-six days later. Edward kept a daily journal of the trip in which he described the terrain and towns they passed through—Cleveland, Columbus, Dayton, Indianapolis, Decatur, Springfield, and other smaller towns. In addition to recording demographic data—population, number of houses, stores, taverns, and so forth—he also reported on the politics of the local newspapers. President Andrew Jackson was the Democratic Party candidate campaigning for reelection; his opponent was Kentucky Senator Henry Clay, the National Republican party candidate.

In 1833 about three hundred people resided in Winchester, living in crude log houses. The surrounding forests provided plenty of timber. There was a water mill for grinding wheat and corn, a tannery to produce leather for shoes and harnesses, a blacksmith and a woodworking shop to make ox carts and farming tools, and a few stores around the town square. Teams of oxen were used for farming, horses and buggies for transportation. Homespun clothing was the regular attire, and coonskin caps were popular. Slowly the surrounding country would be cleared for farming, and the trails transformed into roads for public travel. Illumination at night came from cabin fireplaces or tallow-dip candles.

News traveled slowly. It took weeks for word of Andrew Jackson's election victory over Henry Clay to reach Winchester. Clay's National Republican party soon gave way to the new Whig party, which Miner would actively support.

Miner's previous experience as a shop clerk came in handy in Winchester. He was hired to be the clerk in a two-room log cabin store owned by a St. Louis firm. In the fall of 1833 a stranger came into Miner's store one day. He was a young man who had, like Miner, come a long way—from Canandaigua, New York—to reach Winchester. Like Miner, he had been born in Vermont. With little money and few friends, he sought employment as a schoolteacher in Winchester while he studied to become a lawyer. He was twenty years old, short and slight of build, bright, and ambitious. His name was Stephen A. Douglas.

Miner was impressed with Douglas and decided to help him out. First, he introduced him to several citizens who were starting a new school with forty students, and they hired Douglas to teach there. Secondly, Miner had a stove and a bed in the store's back room, which he offered to share with Douglas. So Edward had a new roommate that winter. Douglas studied his law books at night, and in the spring of 1834 he left Winchester for the larger nearby town of Jacksonville, where he was admitted to the bar. From that humble beginning Douglas's meteoric political career took off: a dozen years later he would become a United States Senator.

Soon Edward was instructed by the creditors of the store's owner to close out the store and sell its stock. He then went to St. Louis in 1834, bought a new stock of goods, and returned to Winchester to start the store anew for himself. Under his ownership and management the business prospered, as the town grew with the arrival of newcomers planning to settle there. One new resident was Sophronia Alden, age twenty-five, who had traveled to Illinois from her home in Ashville, Massachusetts, where her father, Reverend John Alden, a Baptist minister, lived on the family estate. Sophronia had been a student at the school run by Mary Lyon, the persevering advocate of women's education who later founded the seminary that became Mt. Holyoke College. Sophronia made the journey west as a participant in a program to supply well-educated young women to teach in the new towns opening up in the western states. After teaching for a year in nearby Edwardsville, she moved to Winchester in 1833 to teach at the new school.

Perhaps Sophronia inherited her venturesome spirit from a notable forebear. She was a direct descendant of John Alden, a member of the band of Pilgrims who had made history in founding Plymouth in 1620. Alden had married Priscilla Mullins, a courtship fantasized ("Speak for yourself, John") in Henry W. Longfellow's "Courtship of Miles Standish," a lyric poem about the early days of the Pilgrim colony. Thus Edward, by now a prosperous young businessman in Winchester, and Sophronia, the attractive and dedicated new teacher in town, became acquainted, perhaps when Sophronia went shopping at Edward's store. It was not a long courtship; nor did they waste time in starting a family. They were married on April 19, 1834, in Edwardsville, and their first child, James, was born on January 16, 1835.

To meet the needs of his growing business, Miner made trips to Chicago or back east from time to time. On one business trip to New York and Baltimore to buy goods for his store he stopped off in Washington DC, where his congressman took him to the White House to meet President Andrew Jackson. The President was sitting before a fireplace smoking an old corncob pipe and rose from his chair to greet Miner warmly when the congressman introduced him. "I chatted with old gentleman for an hour or so," recalled Miner. That evening the congressman took Miner to a dinner given by Vice President Martin Van Buren: "When we sat down, someone noticed that there were thirteen at the table, which caused a lot of joking."

Edward and Sophronia both attended the Presbyterian Church initially, but when the new Baptist church was built, Sophronia had no difficulty in persuading Edward to become a Baptist and attend the First Baptist Church in Winchester. Edward was a church deacon there for sixty-three years and Sophronia taught Sunday school at the church for decades. Miner was generous in supporting the church's operations and capital needs for construction of a new church and parsonage; he also donated the new bell that called parishioners to worship. He organized the Baptist Church General Association of Illinois, regularly attended their conferences, and contributed generously to Baptist missions and projects at home and abroad. He never declined making some contribution to building a new church, saying he wanted "to place at least a rafter" in it.

Edward G. Miner was a serious man and devout in his faith. It is unlikely that he partook of the whiskey produced at Kilmarnock's local still and sold in the town groceries. To many he was familiarly known as "Deacon" Miner. After he died, the Winchester Times stated, "He was a man of deep religious convictions and was a pioneer of the Baptist organization in this country."

Through his work with the church, Miner met John Mason Peck, a Baptist missionary who had founded Shurtleff College in Alton, Illinois, in 1827. It was the first Baptist college west of the Appalachians, with an enrollment of about ninety students at the time. Miner was a generous benefactor of the small college and a member of its board of trustees for many years.

Miner was appointed U.S. Postmaster in Winchester, 1842–46, and handed out letters through a window in the front door of his store. Miner had prospered as a local merchant, but by 1847 felt it was time to change direction. He sold his store and began accumulating farmlands, some 220 acres, which would surround his new home on West Cherry Street on the outskirts of town. Miner operated the farm for the rest of his life, although personally he engaged in other pursuits, especially banking and public affairs. The Miners lived in the large red brick house with its big, columned front porch for the rest of their lives. They were known for their warm hospitality. Along with the Baptists, Presbyterian preachers stayed at Deacon Miner's house whenever they visited Winchester.

Edward Miner had a favorite expression, "My latch key is never pulled in," and he practiced what he preached.

In 1857 Miner established the first banking house in Winchester, E. G. Miner & Co., which he sold to the First National Bank of Winchester in 1865. Two years later he and two partners started a private banking firm, Miner, Frost, and Hubbard, which he ran until 1886. At the age of seventy-seven, he retired from the bank and other active business interests, having enjoyed considerable success.

Miner took a keen interest in the development of public institutions to meet the growing needs for social services in his county and state, and he represented Scott County, as a Whig, in the Illinois General Assembly from 1846 to 1848. Edward and Sophronia, a former teacher, were both concerned with advancing public school education in Illinois, and in 1839 Edward organized the Scott County public school system and became the first county school commissioner. He also became a trustee and later president of the board of trustees of the Illinois State Hospital for the Insane in Jacksonville.

On February 19, 1858, Abraham Lincoln, the prominent Illinois Republican politician, wrote a letter to Edward G. Miner recommending that he appoint a certain gentleman, Mr. A. G. Sutton, to be superintendent of the addition to the Jacksonville "insane asylum":

> Mr. Sutton is my fellow townsman and friend; and therefore I wish to say for him that he is a man of sterling integrity; and as a master mechanic, or builder, not surpassed by any in our city, or any I have known anywhere, as far as I can judge. I hope you will consider me as being really interested for Mr. Sutton and not as writing this merely to relieve myself of importunity. Please show this to Col. M. Ross [a fellow trustee of the hospital], and let him consider it as intended as much for him as yourself.

The letter is signed, "Your friend as ever, A. Lincoln."

In the course of his public duties and support for the Whigs, and later the Republican party, in Illinois, Miner became acquainted with governors, public officials, and politicians, including Abraham Lincoln. Lincoln, who lived in Springfield, the state capital fifty miles away, was a successful circuit-riding lawyer who had served four terms in the state legislature and one term as a U.S. Congressman. Miner and Lincoln, both the same age, became good, although not close, friends.

III. Abraham Lincoln Comes to Winchester

On August 24, 1854, Abraham Lincoln gave a significant, though little noticed, speech in the Scott County Court House in Winchester. His subject was the Kansas-Nebraska Act, passed in May by the U.S. Congress. In repealing the Missouri Compromise of 1820, the act would allow the citizens of those two territories to decide whether their new states would permit slavery or be free. Democratic Senator Stephen A. Douglas of Illinois, a firm backer of the principle of "popular sovereignty," had introduced the bill and forcefully steered its passage through Congress. However, many antislavery Northerners were incensed over the new act, including Abraham Lincoln, as well as many of Douglas's Democratic followers in Illinois. The senator had returned to his home state to make a series of speeches in Chicago and other northern Illinois towns to defend his position. Lincoln was strongly opposed to the Kansas-Nebraska Act, and passage of the bill had aroused his determination to reenter politics to speak out on the issue about which he felt deeply. He chose a scheduled political meeting of Whig county leaders in Winchester to deliver his first address on the subject.

E. G. Miner's then-twenty-year-old son, James, recalled the event later. As he and his father were walking by the town square, they ran into Nathan M. Knapp, a prominent lawyer and Whig, who had just met with Lincoln and the local U.S. congressman, Richard Yates, at the Aiken House, a Winchester inn. Knapp greeted them and said to James's father, "Miner, Abe Lincoln is over at the Aiken House and wants to see you, He is going to speak in the courthouse this afternoon. He has got up a speech on the Kansas-Nebraska bill which he has never made before, and he has come down here to 'try it on the dog' before he delivers it to larger audiences." E. G. Miner laughed and went over to the inn to greet Yates and Lincoln, who had recently written to Miner to seek his support for election to the United States Senate in the coming session of the state legislature. (At the time each state legislature elected its own senators.) Edward Miner was the Whig candidate for election to the state legislature from his district. (He would be defeated in the general election.) That afternoon, Miner and his son joined about 150 others in the two-story, red brick Scott County courthouse to attend the meeting at which Lincoln would speak.

James later recalled his first glimpse of Abraham Lincoln as he sat on the juror's bench with Congressman Yates, surrounded by prominent local Whigs, including James's father. He was frankly disappointed, expecting him to have a more distinguished appearance, more like the handsome and fashionably dressed congressman. "He was a very tall, ungainly looking man," James recalled. "When he stood up his arms seemed too long for his body, and when he sat down . . . his knees were almost on a plain with his waist. His large, bony face when in repose was unspeakably sad and as unreadable as that of the Sphinx, and his eyes as expressionless as a dead fish. But when he smiled or laughed at one of his own stories or that of another, everything about him changed. His figure became alert; a lightning change came over his countenance, his eyes scintillated, and I thought he had the most expressive features I had ever seen on the face of man."

When the business part of the meeting was completed, the gathering called for Lincoln to speak. He walked over from the juror's bench to address the assembly from in front of the judge's raised platform. James only remembered the main points of his talk, which set forth his reply to Douglas's arguments in favor of the Kansas-Nebraska Act. "He began by telling how in people's minds the Missouri Compromise was held as something sacred," recalled James. This was especially true for the citizens of Illinois, whose senator, Jesse B. Thomas, had introduced the key provision in the bill that would prohibit slavery through-out the Louisiana Purchase territory north of latitude thirty-six degrees, thirty minutes, except for Missouri itself. Lincoln then spoke of the aggressive eager-ness of the Democratic slave-holding party to acquire more slave territory.

The act's supporters declared that it gave equal rights in the settlement of new territories to people from both the North and South. James recalled Lin-coln's words: "Let us see about equal rights of the North and South. How is it in Congressional representation? The South has representation for three-fifths of its slave population in addition to that of their white masters," Lincoln said, referring to the original Constitutional provision in effect at that time. Lincoln then compared the ratio of Congressional representation of a heavily black dis-trict in Georgia where there were five black persons to each white, to that of Winchester's Sixteenth Congressional District. One white man's vote in Georgia was equal to three white men's votes in Illinois. "Talk about equal rights," said Lincoln. "I would like some man to take a pointer dog, and nose around, and snuff about, and see if he can find my rights in such a condition." At that, Lin-coln imitated a dog sniffing about with his head and face, and then laughed. James especially remembered that moment of the speech because, during the rest of it, "[Lincoln] was as earnest and solemn as though he had been deliver-ing a funeral oration. I remember he impressed me with feeling that the country was on the brink of a great disaster."

After Congressman Yates had spoken briefly, Edward G. Miner asked him what he thought of Lincoln's speech. "Miner," he replied, "I have heard this winter all the big men in Congress talk on this question, but Lincoln's is the strongest speech I have ever heard on the subject." After his talk, Lincoln asked Miner and a few other supporters to tell him what they thought of his remarks. One gentleman said that it was a good talk and made some strong points, but that that kind of talk would surely "bust the Whig party wide open." Miner recalled Lincoln's reply: "You're right, I'm afraid it will have to bust." E. G. Miner said later that Lincoln's Winchester speech was his first public address on the Kansas-Nebraska Act; it would serve as a model for his noteworthy talk in Peoria on October 24, 1854, and others leading to the historic Lincoln-Douglas debates on slavery when Lincoln and Stephen A. Douglas were opposing candidates for the U.S. Senate in 1858.

By 1858 the Whig party had dissolved because of internal dissention over the slavery issue stemming from the passage of the Kansas-Nebraska Act. Indeed, the whole country was becoming increasingly bitterly divided over the slavery question. The Northerners opposed to slavery, including many former Whigs like Edward G. Miner, were joining the ranks of the newly formed Republican Party, whose main issue was opposition to the spread of slavery to the western states. In the Presidential election of 1856 the Republicans chose John C. Fremont, the western explorer, to be their candidate. Although James Buchanan, the Democratic candidate, won the election, Fremont won eleven states, a respectable showing for a new party candidate. Abraham Lincoln campaigned actively for the Republican ticket in 1856.

On September 30, 1858, Lincoln, who was now the Republican candidate campaigning for the U.S. Senate against the Democratic incumbent Stephen A. Douglas, returned to Winchester to give another speech. Senator Douglas had spoken a few months earlier before one of the largest crowds ever assembled in Winchester, and had fiercely attacked Lincoln's declaration that "a house divided against itself cannot stand." Lincoln came in from Jacksonville in a carriage drawn by four horses. He was wearing a black suit and calfskin boots and was so covered with dust that it was difficult to recognize him, reported E. G. Miner. The local ladies had prepared a huge barbecue lunch for the out-of-town visitors, and, after washing up, Lincoln was escorted to a special table and enjoyed a hearty meal. He spoke at the county fairgrounds from a covered platform before a crowd of several thousand people from Winchester and surrounding counties, some marching in with flags and bands. Local ladies speedily occupied the seats just in front of the platform, and Judge John Moses, Scott County's first elected judge, introduced the candidate.

Lincoln's talk again focused on his opposition to slavery and its extension in America. He said that he was not an abolitionist, but he would be truly glad if people in the states where slavery existed would enter into measures for gradually doing away with it. He did not wish to interfere with slavery where it was established by law. He had never advocated unconditional emancipation. He also quoted Senator Henry Clay, who had declared that slavery was a great moral and political evil. "The Republicans think that slavery is socially wrong. The Democrats, on the other hand, believe that slavery is right," said Lincoln. The pro-slavery policy of the Democratic party, unless unchecked, would nationalize slavery before long. Lincoln spoke for two hours in his "usual cool, unimpassioned, logical manner," said Miner, and received three rousing cheers at the end. Some ardent Republicans, however, were hoping for a more enthusiastic response by the crowd, Miner reported.

Late that afternoon, Miner called on Lincoln, who was staying at the Haggard Hotel. He found him stretched out full-length on the bed in his room, resting before a reception at the hotel that evening. Miner asked him how he thought the November election would turn out and recorded Lincoln's reply. "I think," said Lincoln, "the northern part of the state will be all right, with a good prospect of carrying the central and southern parts, if the Democrats do not send into these districts too many corn-cutters from Kentucky and Indiana." Lincoln was well-liked in Winchester, which had been part of his congressional district when he was a congressman. But there were many folks in the area formerly from Kentucky and other southern states who were ardent supporters of Senator Douglas in the upcoming election. The "Little Giant" was very popular in Winchester and nearby towns.

At the reception that evening, a reporter noted Lincoln's sure political touch as he greeted people with a kindly nod or friendly word. A shy old lady from the country wearing a sun bonnet left happy and pleased with his informal, "Howdy, Auntie." A lady in more formal attire was greeted with, "Glad to meet you, Madam. I hope you are well." Lincoln, a veteran of the Black Hawk War in 1832, recognized several of his former comrades-in-arms when they came down the receiving line. "Howdy, Mose, I remember you being with Colonel Leib's regiment," was his greeting to one veteran; "I remember you well, saw you when you came in from Stillman's defeat," to another. The reporter was impressed with Lincoln's phenomenal memory of faces and events.

Lincoln spent two days and nights in Winchester before going on to his next engagement in Pittsfield, and E. G. Miner invited him to make use of a back room at the Miner bank, which Lincoln did. Miner later recalled that he and Lincoln had a friendly talk there about the breakup of the Whig party and the future of the Republican party. On his second evening in Winchester Lincoln gave another talk at the Court House. Lincoln discussed the slavery issue and especially the general sentiment that had prevailed in America when the Constitution was adopted in 1787, and Miner noted his remarks. He stated that the founders of our government believed that, sooner or later, slavery would be removed and therefore did not permit the word "slave" to be used in the Constitution. They felt that it would be a disgrace for such a word to appear in the constitution of a government that had declared that "all men are free and equal" in its Declaration of Independence. Miner also noted that Lincoln attracted far less attention at the hotel or in the streets than had Senator Douglas on his visit to Winchester. In November the Democratic majority in the Illinois state legislature reelected Stephen A. Douglas to the United States Senate.

About a year later, Edward G. Miner was discussing politics with a half dozen Republican state officials in a corner of the rotunda of the state house in Springfield when Lincoln came in leading his young son, Tad. Seeing Miner, Lincoln remembered an episode from his visit to Winchester the previous year. Miner later recalled his words:

> Our friend Miner here, gentlemen, reminds me of a visit I made to his town of Winchester. I will have to tell a joke on myself. Douglas had been there a little while before me and made a speech. When I was canvassing the state last year, at Winchester I stopped at Haggard Hotel . . . and as I had no appointment for the next day, I stayed in Winchester. In the morning I walked up to the square to get shaved, and a little Irishman came walking along with me, and he said, "Ah, Mr. Lincoln, and you made a foine speech yesterday, and so ya did. I never heard the loikes of it before." [And Lincoln went on mimicking the Irishman.] And after that he says, "And now Mr. Lincoln, could you give a quarter to buy my breakfast?"
>
> And Lincoln said he told the fellow he was afraid he wanted to buy whiskey with it. "No, indade he didn't. So I gave him the quarter. After getting shaved, I went back to the hotel. There was a big crowd in the street chasing the Griggsville band, which was about to start home, and as I got among them they cried, 'Three cheers for Lincoln!' And it was given and then someone yelled out, 'And now three cheers for Douglas!' and I looked around and it was the same fellow I gave the quarter to."

"As he told it," recalled Miner, "Mr. Lincoln laughed heartily, and we all joined in."

IV. The Country Doctor

Edward Griffith Miner died in 1900 at the age of ninety-one, and Chicago, St. Louis, and several downstate newspapers published obituaries and tributes about him. The *Winchester Standard* said:

> E. G. Miner more than any other in this community has been the living link between the two extremes of this century. He had trod the humble paths of social, domestic, and religious duties in those pioneer days. He had a powerful hand in the achievement in civil government and constitutional freedom, and these personal experiences were brought to us with all the vivid distinctness of a clear, strong memory. He was one of the few pioneers who kept pace with the progress of this wonderful period. . . .
>
> He is among the last of those great spirits of our heroic age to join the larger circle on the brighter shore. He had left us the halo of the true character of a Christian gentleman and an American patriot to be cherished and revered.

In 1832 Edward G. Miner had arrived by horse and wagon in the little frontier community of Winchester, whose population had grown from three hundred to seventeen hundred in 1900. By the turn of the century when Miner died, he had both witnessed and contributed significantly to the development and progress of his hometown and state.

Edward and Sophronia Miner had six children. The oldest was James, born in Winchester on January 16, 1835. James was later described by his son, Edward, as the "beloved family physician of that region, never caring to go elsewhere, though he had many tempting offers because of his reputation as a diagnostician." After local schooling, James became a four-year student at Shurtleff College in Alton, from which he graduated in 1854. He taught school for a year in Griggsville and then entered Mc Dowell's College, the medical school of the University of Missouri in St. Louis. During summers he trained in the office of a local physician, Dr. Clark Roberts, whom he later described as a character "of great originality and of a quality which was an inspiration to any embryo doctor."

After completing his course at the university, Dr. Miner established his practice with two other doctors in 1856 at Waverly, Illinois, not far from Springfield. After four years, Miner decided he needed further training and entered Jefferson Medical College in Philadelphia, from which he graduated in 1861.

In April 1861 Dr. Miner married Eleanor Hawthorne Thomas, age twenty-five, daughter of Judge and Mrs. J. R. Thomas, who came originally from a parish near New Orleans, where Eleanor was born. She also had New England roots, however: her second cousin was the popular novelist Nathaniel Hawthorne. When Eleanor was a child the family moved to Illinois, and had finally settled in the small town of Godfrey. Eleanor attended Monticello Seminary, the well-regarded school for young women in Godfrey. The family later moved to Waverly, where she met the young practicing physician, Dr. James Miner. The Miners had seven children, although their firstborn, Willard, died in childhood. Their next child, Edward G. Miner II, named after his grandfather, was born on December 19, 1863, in the midst of the Civil War, just one month after President Abraham Lincoln delivered the Gettysburg Address to dedicate the military cemetery on the bloodstained Pennsylvania battlefield.

Like his father, James took an active interest in public affairs and the politics of the day. When he moved to Waverly in 1856, he reported that, on his visits to Springfield, he met Abraham Lincoln a number of times. Lincoln almost always inquired about James's father, E. G. Miner, along with two other prominent Winchester citizens. The last time James Miner saw Lincoln in Springfield was about a week after Lincoln's election as President. They met on the street as James was walking toward the Wabash Railroad depot, and he congratulated the President-elect on his victory.

When he was studying at medical school in Philadelphia, James attended a reception at the Continental Hotel in February 1861 for the President-elect, who was on his way to Washington DC for his inauguration. The next day, James heard him make a stirring and notable speech at Independence Hall in which he declared, "I never had a feeling, politically, that did not spring from the sentiments embodied in the Declaration of Independence." That was the last time James saw Abraham Lincoln alive. In April 1865 in Springfield he attended the funeral services of the great President whom he and his father had also known as a good neighbor in Illinois. James joined the thousands who filed through the state house to view Lincoln's remains on a catafalque. Some years later, he wrote, "People of the present day have but little idea of the profound grief, great loss, and utter helplessness that the people of that time felt in the death of Mr. Lincoln. I saw many strong men shed tears and heard many women cry out loud."

After graduating from Jefferson Medical College, James returned to his medical practice in Waverly. Following the outbreak of the Civil War in April 1861, President Lincoln authorized a national recruitment program to enlist soldiers for the Union army. James Miner was commissioned as first assistant surgeon in the 101st Infantry Regiment of Illinois Volunteers, which was formally mustered into the U.S. Army in September 1862. After training, the regiment was transported to Davis Mills, Mississippi, where it was assigned to the Army of Tennessee, commanded by General Ulysses S. Grant. Around this time James received the sad news that his younger brother, John Howard Miner, a Union soldier in the Thirty-Third Illinois Volunteers, had already been killed in the Mississippi campaign in September, when a Mississippi steam boat carrying Union troops was ambushed by the Confederates near Helena, Arkansas.

James Miner's regiment then marched to Lumpkin Mills, Mississippi. According to Miner's account, he had become progressively debilitated by rheumatic fever. There had been a great deal of sickness in the regiment when it was training in Cairo, Illinois, in November, and many men had been discharged or died from disease. Miner stayed in a large mansion in Lumpkin Mills during the month of December. The men of the family that owned the house had joined the Confederate Army and gone off to war, leaving the daughter and a young male cousin to look after the place. They graciously took in Dr. Miner and cared for him during his illness.

On November 30, Miner's regiment moved six miles away to Holly Springs, an important railway junction forty miles from Memphis near the northern border of the state. Grant had chosen the town as his headquarters and the staging area from which to launch his overland campaign against Vicksburg, and the Union army had amassed a huge supply depot there. On December 20, Confederate General Earl Van Dorn swept down on Holly Springs with three cavalry brigades in a bold attack. He forced the garrison to surrender, took hundreds of Union prisoners, drove off the other defenders, and seized or destroyed Union supplies of arms, ammunition, and other equipment. After two more days of destruction, Van Dorn's forces, pursued by Union cavalry, abandoned Holly Springs. The raid forced Grant, who had advanced south to Oxford, to delay his Vicksburg campaign and return to Holly Springs. Without supplies, he was unable to continue his push south to Vicksburg.

Dr. Miner recorded the following account of a meeting with General Grant at his headquarters in Holly Springs. Five of the 101st companies had lost all their tents and blankets in the Van Dorn raid, and the colonel in charge requested Miner, only partially weakened by the fever, to bring a requisition for these supplies to General Grant's Chief Quartermaster, Colonel Mills. Mills said he could not fill the order, but a special train was going to Memphis the next day to obtain supplies requested by Grant, and he suggested that Miner try to see Grant himself.

Miner rode to Grant's headquarters, located in a handsome mansion, and upon entering was surprised to meet one of his former classmates at Shurtleff College, Henry Bowers, who was now serving as Grant's adjutant. They exchanged pleasantries, and Bowers introduced Miner as his "good friend" to Colonel Rawlins, Grant's chief of staff. Miner stated his case to the officers, and Rawlins escorted him into Grant's office and introduced him to the general. Grant was working on some papers at a small desk before a blazing fire.

"Be seated. I'll see you," said the general, rising to shake Miner's hand. He resumed his writing, all the while vigorously smoking a cigar in short, jerky puffs. Every now and then he leaned back in his chair and blew away the clouds of smoke that filled the space around him. "Well, Doctor, what is it?" Grant inquired abruptly.

"Five companies of our regiment, General, were up on Coldwater and lost all their tents. They retreated and joined Colonel O'Mara's regiment and were not taken by Van Dorn," Miner replied.

"Yes, I know; they acted bravely," said the general.

"I have requisitions for tents, but Colonel Mills says he can't fill them and has sent me to you," continued Miner.

"Certainly they shall have tents. Hand me the requisitions." Grant signed all three copies.

Miner took the requisitions back to Colonel Mills, who was surprised, remarking, "That's the first time I ever saw Grant's signature to a colonel's requisition!" Miner wondered if he would actually get the tents. "Certainly," the colonel shot back, and the next day the tents arrived from Memphis.

Meanwhile, there was still some skirmishing going on between the two sides in the area, some of it quite close to the house where Miner was living in Lumpkin Mills. One day he was standing in the doorway observing the military action, when two Confederate soldiers came to the house and said they had orders to take him prisoner. He was quite weak and lame at the time, still recovering from a three-week bout of rheumatic fever, and pleaded with his captors to be released. Miner later recalled the incident: "I told them it wasn't the practice to take surgeons prisoners. They said they had orders to take everyone to a certain place. I told them to take me to some of their generals or colonels." Walking down the street at the Confederate base, supported by his captors because of his lameness, Miner met Captain Phil Price, a Confederate officer, with whom he had attended lectures on anatomy at McDowell's College in St. Louis when he was a medical student there. Miner recalled: "Hailing him, he at once recognized me, and I asked him if he took surgeons prisoner. He said, 'Well, I'll make an exception in your case. Where do you wish to go?'" Miner was released and, disabled by sickness, was discharged from the U.S. Army in January 1863. He returned to his medical practice in Waverly. One Miner son had already given his life for his country. Perhaps Miner figured that that was enough.

In 1868, the Miners went back to Winchester to live, and James continued his medical practice there until he retired. Dr. Carl E. Black, from the neighboring town of Jacksonville, knew Dr. Miner well and, after Miner's death, described his career as a country doctor in the *Illinois Medical Journal*. James, he remarked, like his father, had "elected to devote his life and energy to a small community."

Dr. Miner served on committees of the Illinois State Medical Society and attended meetings of the American Medical Association as the Society's delegate. He was a founder of the Morgan County Medical Society when he lived in Waverly, and he helped to organize, and later became president of, the Scott County Medical Society when his family moved to Winchester. He treated all his fellow citizens of Winchester, the poor as well as people of means, and he knew the country doctor's life of dark night rides and bedside vigils.

"He was a constant reader of medical literature . . . who enjoyed the progress medicine was making and appreciated it," Dr. Black wrote. He also "had a natural capacity and desire to keep abreast of the best medical thought of the times, and was always inquiring as to the value of these advances and ready and anxious to apply them for the benefit of his patients." Dr. Black noted that Miner's broad knowledge of medicine made him especially popular with the young doctors with whom he liked to associate.

When James Miner began to practice medicine, most doctors were general practitioners as well as surgeons and specialists, and so was he. Quinine and calomel were the medicines he regularly prescribed. Progress in medical research and practice developed rapidly over the span of Miner's career, and James "easily parted with the old and accepted the new"—the clinical laboratory, the x-ray, the trained nurse, and the modern hospital. Said Dr. Black, "I have talked with Dr. Miner many times and know that he was a close and enthusiastic follower of all the changes in the understanding of disease."

James was a voracious reader and well informed on the topics of the day. He was especially interested in the history of his country and the region where he lived, and his library was filled with historic letters, pictures, and books. It also contained the yellowing volumes of a small set of Shakespeare, which had been carried by his father on his wagon trek from Middlebury, Vermont, to Winchester. James's son, Edward G. Miner II, had the run of his father's library and inherited his father's love of history and passion for books and reading. Describing Dr. Miner's personality, Dr. Black stated, "He was genial and frank, but with a sense of humor which sometimes suggested cynicism, although never disagreeable. When occasion demanded, he could be most positive."

Dr. James Miner and his family had moved into his father's Winchester farmhouse after he died in 1900, and James died in the same house in 1925, at the age of ninety, surrounded by his family. A little while before he died he wrote in a letter to his son, Edward, "The Lord has been mighty good to me, far beyond my desserts, and beyond some dark passages in my life, this world has been a mighty fine world for me to live in. I have enjoyed my life and the friends I have found in it. I have lived in the love of my family. I have been proud of my children. So far as I am concerned, I would not want to live in a better world."

Figure 1. The author by a monument honoring Thomas Minor, a founder of Stonington, Connecticut, in 1653 and the first member of the family to come to America.

Figure 2. Edward G. Miner (1809–1900) settled in Winchester, Illinois, in 1832.

Figure 3. Dr. James Miner (1835–1925), "the country doctor" in Winchester and Ned Miner's father.

Figure 4. Miner home in Winchester, built in 1847. Photo courtesy of Department of Rare Books and Special Collections, University of Rochester Libraries.

Pfaudler Company's Plant, Rochester, N. Y.

Largest Glass-Enameled Steel Tank Factory in the World--One of the Largest and Most Modernly Equipped Factories in the United States.

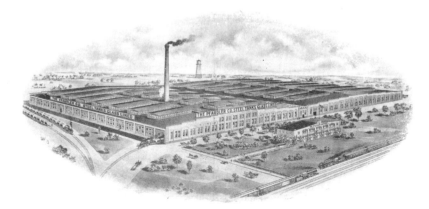

Figure 5. The new Pfaudler Company plant in Rochester, 1909.

Figure 6. Edward G. Miner II (1863–1955), known as Ned, became president of the Rochester Chamber of Commerce in 1910 and president of the Pfaudler Company in 1911. Photo courtesy of Department of Rare Books and Special Collections, University of Rochester Libraries.

Figure 7. University of Rochester Alumni Association Dinner, 1942. Edward
G. Miner, chairman of the Board of Trustees; Alan Valentine, president; and
Kenneth Keating, president of the Alumni Association (and later U.S. Senator
from New York).

Figure 8. Edward G. Miner receives the Rochester Civic Medal in 1940 from Mayor Samuel B. Dicker (left) as *New York Times* science editor Waldemar B. Kaempffert looks on.

Figure 9. Helen Ranlet Miner promoted worthy causes at ladies' teas.

Figure 10. Elinor Miner Lamont, daughter of Helen R. Miner and Edward G. Miner.

Figure 11. Edward G. Miner with son Ranlet Miner (left) and grandson Edward Miner Lamont holding great grandson Edward Miner Lamont Jr., 1954.

V. Ned Miner Comes to Rochester

Edward Griffith Miner II, known as Ned Miner, later wrote of his boyhood. His best friend was John A. McKeene, who later became Judge of the District Court in Scott County. In the summer, barefoot, they tramped along the creeks, small lakes, and sloughs, and went fishing and swimming. In the fall they gathered wild grapes, mulberries, blackberries, raspberries, pecans, hazelnuts, butternuts, and walnuts—all the wild berries and nuts that grew in the nearby countryside. Winchester was just a few miles east of the rolling hills on the bluffs overlooking the Illinois River and fifty miles east of Hannibal, Missouri, the home of Mark Twain, who wrote the classic story *Tom Sawyer* about the adventures of a boy growing up in those parts.

Ned attended the local elementary school and high school, supplementing his education from the books in his father's and grandfather's libraries, which naturally contained the Bible and classics like Shakespeare's plays and sonnets, Sir Thomas Moore's *Urn Burial*, and the works of Victor Hugo. Looking back years later, Ned was not impressed with the schooling he received in the small country town of Winchester. One teacher of physics and geometry taught him "what was best of all—to think." At home his parents taught him some Greek and Latin. "But my education, if I have any, has come from reading, all my life," he declared later.

When he was sixteen Ned worked in a local brickyard; at seventeen he took a job as a night telegrapher at the Winchester station of the Chicago, Burlington, and Quincy Railroad. He retained an avid interest and enthusiasm for railroading throughout his life, and years later became a director on the board of the Buffalo, Rochester, and Pittsburgh Railroad. He also dabbled with the idea of becoming a schoolteacher and took the Scott County examinations to obtain a Teacher's Certificate, scoring a commendable scholarship average of 96.5. Nevertheless, Ned decided that the life of a "railroad man," going to college, and teaching were not for him. The world of business in that era of America's burgeoning economic growth offered the fastest path to building a personal fortune and earning the respect of his fellow citizens. He was anxious to get going, and his small hometown in the farming country of Illinois was not the place to achieve his goals.

In 1883, at the age of nineteen, Ned Miner left Winchester to visit his cousin Charles C. Puffer in Rochester, New York. Puffer was one of the founders of a new enterprise that was just getting organized; it later became the Pfaudler Company. He asked Ned to become his private secretary, and Ned accepted. The company's plan was to manufacture containers to be used for holding perishable liquids and foods instead of those currently made from wood, metal, or other materials that were unsuitable for that purpose. Pfaudler would produce glass-enameled steel tanks, based on a process developed by the Rochester inventor Caspar Pfaudler, whose work had patent protection in the U.S. and other countries.

The early years of the enterprise were a period of tense anxiety for the founders and Ned. The "risk of failure" was real, Ned wrote to his father. For Ned Miner, to succeed meant hard work, long hours, and no vacations. In 1884 Miner became secretary of the company. In those days before the typewriter was commonly used in offices, he wrote out all of the company's correspondence longhand, often staying late at night to work and sleeping on a couch in the firm's office in the Powers Building.

Ned wrote home often, usually to his father, and was eager to receive letters and news from his family. His small town and churchgoing parents and grandparents were naturally concerned about the new direction their oldest son and grandson had abruptly chosen for his life. In an 1884 letter to Ned his devout grandmother Sophronia Miner prayed "that you may resist temptation" and "walk in the narrow path." She added that she was glad to hear that Ned had made so many friends, "but you must not let those whose purses are longer than yours draw too freely, as you have no rich father to whom you can resort for aid."

A "long purse" was exactly what Ned was seeking for himself. He wrote his father that he was "impatient for money, big money," and that "it chafed not to be where [his] say would have deciding weight and the measure of reward." In another letter home, he wrote, "Don't worry about my affairs. I'm not dead yet. I'll make my pile pretty soon or bust a blood vessel." Ned Miner believed he had the ability to manage the company successfully. "A fellow must sound his trumpet and ride over someone or someone will ride over him." Later, he wrote, "I'll make a barrel of money or turn up my toes from overwork—one or the other." Ned planned to "work like the devil" and "land my pile by forty-five or fifty." Years later Miner described his work ethic: "Learn to work. That is the thing that seems to have been lost sight of today—the joy of working. But no man can succeed who does not love work for itself." Ned was also, however, beginning to enjoy leading a young-man-about-town lifestyle that was unfamiliar and probably perplexing to his parents.

In 1902 the Pfaudler Vacuum Fermentation Company was reconstituted as the Pfaudler Company and made a public offering of a $250,000 issue of 6 percent preferred shares. The founders' group held the common stock with a par value of $650,000. Edward G. Miner was listed as vice president and one of the five directors on the Pfaudler board. The existing machinery from a plant in Detroit was moved to Lincoln Park in Rochester, where the company's new plant and warehouse, occupying five acres, was constructed in 1903. The brewery industry was a prime customer for Pfaudler, because of the company's newly developed sectional type of glass-lined steel tanks.

The folks back home began taking note of Ned Miner's successful career in Rochester. The 1903 Standard Atlas of Scott County, Illinois, reminded its readers of Ned's distinguished Winchester roots, reported his business accomplishments, and listed the corporate and charitable organizations which engaged him as a director or trustee. The atlas also noted the social clubs that he had joined, including the Rochester Athletic Club, the Genesee Valley Club, the Rochester Yacht Club, the Rochester Historical Society, where he had read several papers, and Company A, Boys in Blue, the local Republican club. Said the atlas, "The real Scott County Boy who makes a success in other fields gives the credit to the common-sense views of life and wholesome experience he gained from its citizens in his youth, and Mr. Miner is no exception to the rule."

Miner devoted much of his time to Pfaudler's sales efforts, introducing Pfaudler products to prospective customers and nailing down orders. By 1904 he had built up a sales force of nine men who reported to him. He was on the road constantly, traveling by train all over the country to cities with breweries. His files are filled with handwritten letters written on hotel stationery back to the head office in Rochester requesting engineering advice, cost estimates, and other data.

While attending a brewers' convention in St. Louis, Ned narrowly escaped a deadly accident. He was caught between two streetcars going opposite directions and was badly squeezed and rolled, suffering two broken collarbones, two broken ribs, a deep gash on his head, and sprained arms. He recovered from his painful injuries at St. Luke's Hospital in St. Louis.

Ned undertook another initiative of great benefit to the company in its early years. Recognizing the importance of conducting research to improve Pfaudler's manufacturing processes and develop new products, he established a research unit at the plant in 1907 headed by a member of the Cornell University chemistry department faculty. Its contributions would prove to be of tremendous value.

Ned Miner's ambition, brains, and work ethic paid off. Elected vice president of Pfaudler in 1902, he added the title of general manager four years later, and in 1911 Edward G. Miner succeeded Charles Puffer to become president of the Pfaudler Company. He was forty-eight years old.

In 1911 the company's first venture into the dairy industry led to a significant expansion of its business. Two large glass-lined tanks were mounted on a railway car operated by the Boston and Maine Railroad for the Whiting Milk Company of Boston. After the passage of the U.S. Pure Food and Drug laws in 1906, sanitary and easy-to-clean tanks were needed for food and dairy products, and glass-lined steel was ideal for this purpose. Miner soon became a director of the National Dairy Association and a member of two other dairy trade associations.

The enactment of the Prohibition Act in 1919 ended Pfaudler's American brewery business, an added incentive for Ned Miner, as the company's president, to increase efforts to focus on new industries. With the growth of the chemical industry, Pfaudler scientists provided the acid-resistant material needed for chemical processing and storage vessels. Pfaudler also pioneered ways to fabricate and weld stainless steel for use in the food and dairy industries, and its engineers developed specialized machinery for new industries, like pharmaceuticals, and new uses, like putting orange juice in cans.

The growth of Pfaudler's operations continued steadily as the company became the world's leading manufacturer of glass-lined steel tanks. The company's tanks were manufactured in four plants—in Rochester; Elyria, Ohio; Germany; and Scotland—which Miner called on regularly. He was visiting the Pfaudler plant in Schwetzingen, Germany, in August 1914 when Germany, at the start of World War I, invaded Belgium and imposed martial law throughout Germany. He returned a year later to check up on the plant's status, even amid the turbulent wartime conditions. The devastating war in Europe, which led to the American entry in 1917, ended further overseas travel until the war was over.

During the 1920s the company continued to develop its worldwide sales organization, and Pfaudler tanks, tank trucks, and freight cars for shipping milk and other products were exported around the world. Large dairies in New Zealand stored their milk in Pfaudler tanks and a brewery in Australia used hundreds of them.

During the Great Depression, however, orders for Pfaudler products fell off. The company cut salaries by 10 percent and halved the common stock dividend in 1931. The slowdown would continue until the national defense buildup before Pearl Harbor and the U.S. entry into World War II, which would provide new business opportunities for Pfaudler.

During World War II, Rochester's technologically oriented companies were fully employed with a large number of government orders for military equipment and materials, and the Pfaudler Company received the Army-Navy E Production Award for its contribution to the war effort. At the award ceremony, General Ray L. Avery especially commended the firm for producing devices used in manufacturing penicillin, a new compound used to combat infection. Pfaudler made another key contribution to the war effort. After the Japanese closed off most of the supplies of natural rubber to the U.S., American chemical companies met the challenge by developing synthetic rubber. Pfaudler designed and produced the high-pressure vessels needed to process this new material.

Edward G. Miner served as president of the Pfaudler Company until 1931, when, at the age of sixty-eight, he relinquished the office to become Chairman of the Board of Directors, a position he held until his death in 1955. Until late in life, Miner attended the board meetings of the parent firm and its seven subsidiaries, including three in Europe, except when travel was restricted during both World Wars. During the years of Miner's leadership, the company's operations expanded dramatically. By the 1950s the Rochester plant alone employed thirteen hundred people.

Ned Miner traveled overseas frequently—at least twenty trans-Atlantic voyages to Europe, plus trips to South America, Australia, China, and Japan—to visit Pfaudler's manufacturing and sales operations. He spent many months abroad developing Pfaudler's business in the principal world markets. His colleagues especially praised his marketing skills in introducing Pfaudler products to new customers and to markets at home and abroad. Mercer Brugler, who succeeded Miner as president of Pfaudler, said years later that the fact that Pfaudler was a worldwide company with plants in Europe and Asia and sales branches all around the world was owed largely to Miner's "genius." Along with sound management and strategic planning, Ned Miner's wit and charm contributed to his success in business. It also did in affairs of the heart.

Charles W. Ranlet was a prominent citizen of Holyoke, Massachusetts, president of the Hadley Falls National Bank, and noted for his beautiful collection of two hundred varieties of roses adorning the grounds of his home. He also was a substantial investor in the Pfaudler Company in its early days, and his son Robert had started working there. This connection brought Ned Miner and Ranlet's pretty daughter, Helen, together, which led to their blossoming romance.

The Holyoke Evening Telegram's announcement of the engagement of Edward G. Miner to Helen B. Ranlet of Holyoke stated that Miner was "one of the most popular young club men of Rochester, where he was well known as a business man with a wide circle of friends. Miss Ranlet is the belle of Holyoke and pretty as a picture." Ned Miner, thirty-six, and Helen Ranlet, twenty-nine, were married on April 26, 1900, in Holyoke. Five hundred people filled the Second Congregational Church to witness the marriage ceremony, in which the Episcopal service was used. The society reporter covering the event gushed, "The bride looked divinely fair in a gown of rich satin duchess and wore a veil of white tulle." He described the wedding as "the most brilliant society event in Holyoke" in a long time.

The address of the Miners' newly built house in Rochester, which was designed by Rochester architect Claude Bragdon and completed in 1906, was 2 Argyle Street, on the corner of Argyle and fashionable East Avenue. St. Paul's Episcopal Church on East Avenue, which the Miners attended, was a few blocks downtown from their house. So was the George Eastman House, the spectacular home of the inventor and founder of Eastman Kodak, the world's leading camera and film manufacturer. After Eastman's death, the mansion was converted in 1949 to a museum. Further down East Avenue was the Rochester Gas and Electric building, where, some years later, E. G. Miner would have an office on the tenth floor.

Miner rode to the office in a glossy black, box-shaped electric car with green trim, which he continued to use for short city runs long after other automobiles of this type had disappeared from the streets of Rochester. Later on his garage would house a big, black, chauffeur-driven Pierce Arrow limousine for longer trips.

The Miner children—daughter Elinor, born in 1901, followed by son Ranlet in 1902—grew up in the large, three-story red brick house with their parents, who would live there for the rest of their lives. Ned Miner's favorite room in the house was his library, just off the central staircase, where he would spend countless hours reading and writing. The wall space was largely taken up by tall bookcases that stored his extensive collection of books and manuscripts, which he steadily added to over the years. A business executive remarked, when E. G. Miner was appointed chairman of the board of trustees of the University of Rochester, "Ned Miner makes me mad. No matter what subject I bring up, he knows more about it than I do." Henry Clune, a columnist for Rochester's *Democrat and Chronicle* agreed: "A man of charm, culture, and wit, Mr. Miner all his life has had an insatiable curiosity about the human comedy and the actors who perform upon its infinite stage. He has been an omnivorous reader, and his knowledge of a wide variety of subjects has astonished his friends."

Miner gave a number of talks and wrote numerous articles that attest to his wide-ranging intellectual curiosity. His venues ranged from the Rochester Engineering Society to the Chamber of Commerce to two men's dining clubs with a penchant for scholarly discourse, the Fortnightly Club and the Pundit Club, where he gave some fifteen talks over the years. Among the many subjects he chose were *Yellow Fever, The Shipwreck and Wanderings of Alvar Nunez Cabeza de Vaca, Inflation, Its Effect on Selling, Seward's Diplomacy in Our Civil War, French Loans During Our Revolutionary War, Commercial Aviation*, and *Leisure*.

Sometimes he told stories about his trips to foreign countries. One time after returning from Mexico, he was asked if he had attended a bullfight in Mexico City. "Yes, I saw one and never care to see another," was Ned's reply. He was appalled by the bloody butchery of the spectacle in which two horses had been gored and killed. A rich and varied menu of topics—history, business, economics, politics, and philosophy—informed and entertained his audiences.

A subject of special interest to Miner was the origin of Mormonism in upstate New York. In his early years in Rochester he had talked with people who had known Joseph Smith, the first Mormon leader, or had learned about him from those who knew him. Miner collected rare books and pamphlets on the early days of Mormonism, and wrote a paper on the subject that he delivered before the Pundit Club. "Its Judea was the vicinity of Palmyra, New York, and its prophet and high priest bore the good old American name of Smith," wrote Miner.

These meetings took place at club members' houses or at various Rochester clubs, such as the Genesee Valley Club or the Country Club. A letter from Ned Miner to a University of Rochester geology professor illustrates his approach in recruiting speakers:

My Dear Doctor Fairchild,

This is merely a formal reminder of my request that you do me the kindness to prepare a paper for the Pundit Club, which is to meet at my house, No. 2 Argyle Street, on April 6th, 1920.

You know, of course, that some of us are ignorant of anything except the laws of trade, and that our terminology is that of the counting house: but we are, I think, all of us keenly interested in the great work you have done, and anxious to hear of it, so be kind to us in that respect, and deal with our starved intellects in such a way that we can understand it.

With many thanks for your courtesy in this matter and with the keen expectation of the pleasure, which is to come, I am

Yours very truly,
E. G. Miner

In 1908, on a business trip to South America, Miner saw firsthand the ravages wrought by yellow fever. He did much reading on the subject and began acquiring an extensive collection of books and pamphlets on yellow fever. Perhaps remembering his father's treatment of patients suffering from sickness and fevers emanating from the Illinois River bottom country also aroused his interest in the subject. When the University of Rochester Medical Library was established, he made a gift of forty-one volumes on yellow fever to the new library and continued to purchase new material for the collection as it became available.

Miner was an astute book collector, visiting bookshops on his business travels abroad as well as in the U.S. He made a number of gifts of rare books to the University of Rochester Library, including first editions and manuscripts of several outstanding nineteenth-century American authors—James Russell Lowell, Oliver Wendell Holmes, and John Greenleaf Whittier. His interest in American history led him to collect and donate to the library scarce publications on the Civil War, the history of the states of New York and Illinois, and volumes on early American transportation.

in hope and work, remembering that a noble, logical diagram once recorded will never die," proclaimed Burnham.

When Ned had first arrived in Rochester in 1883, horse-drawn carriages, horse cars, and wagons crowded the downtown city streets. Pedestrians, bicyclists, and horses tied to hitching posts at the curb added to the din and confusion of the street traffic. A decade later, electric trolleys helped relieve the congestion, although in the early years they caused injuries and deaths before more safe operating procedures and mechanisms were introduced. Ned would not forget his own close call in his trolley accident in St. Louis. Still later, the public would be driving their new Model-T Fords and other automobiles through the city streets. (Ned Miner bought his first Woods Electric car in 1911.) The city was expanding, with rows of neat, single-family homes, often with small gardens, on tree-shaded streets extending out from the downtown center. The changing modes of transportation and spreading growth of the city clearly demanded careful planning to design the streets, parkways, and parking to accommodate the new flows of traffic.

Ned Miner, as president of the Chamber of Commerce, took the lead in persuading his fellow members to adopt sound, professional approaches to city planning to guide the future development of his hometown. In May 1910, at the Chamber's initiative, the second National Conference of City Planning met in Rochester, spurring enthusiasm for city beautification and municipal improvements among Rochester's citizens. Miner, a strong advocate of city planning, was also a member of the Civic Improvement Committee, appointed by the Chamber. In 1910 this committee decided to hire three leading planning experts to prepare a plan for Rochester's future development. Having pressed the committee to take action, Ned worked hard at soliciting donations to pay for the study.

He also recognized the importance of selling the idea of good planning to his fellow citizens, which he went about with letters and talks to local groups. In a 1911 article in *The Common Good,* a progressive local periodical, he stated that he was unequivocally in favor of a city plan, "but I base my advocacy on grounds of economy. If in carrying out such schemes, a beautiful city should incidentally result, I shall not be displeased." He proposed that the city should purchase land to accommodate future growth, build streets parallel to Main Street for greater traffic efficiency, and recognize the banks of the Genesee River, which flowed through the city, as one of the city's most valuable assets. He said that he had preached about the economic benefits of the plan, bearing in mind the concerns of taxpayers about the costs. "And yet," he said, "I am a dreamer when I look at this city of the future. There are few cities in the world that have greater natural beauty than this, and I know that sometime this city will come into its own."

Charles M. Robinson of Rochester, a nationally recognized planning expert and head of the Civic Improvement Committee, was impressed with Miner's vision and leadership in the city planning campaign and wrote to him, stating, "I am just longing for the time when I can vote for you for Mayor." The initial enthusiasm of most citizens over the new city plan when it was first made public, however, did not last long. By 1914 the city administration had rejected almost all of the major recommendations in the planning study. Controversy over the proposed location of civic buildings and streets, politics, and the projected high costs doomed the key elements of the plan, and the Civic Improvement Committee, which had commissioned the study, was dissolved. It was frustrating for Ned, but he didn't give up.

City planning in Rochester went forward, dealing with more modest projects and traffic regulations on a piecemeal basis, and Ned Miner was an active member of several committees, private citizens' groups, and official boards that dealt with planning. The automobile population in Rochester had grown from zero in 1900 to 110,000 in 1929, requiring periodic review of traffic patterns and street alterations. In 1929 Miner was one of three private citizens on the five-man City Planning Board charged with approving, upgrading, or developing new projects—subdivisions, street changes, parking areas, railroad-grade crossings, parks, and bridges over the Genesee River and Erie Canal—and making recommendations. The board met every two weeks in the City Hall Annex.

In April the board agreed to retain a St. Louis urban planning firm, Harland Bartholomew and Associates, to prepare a comprehensive city plan for Rochester. Ned Miner was an active participant in the board's deliberations over the draft report, and was especially critical of the section dealing with railroad lines and terminals serving Rochester. He had long had a special interest in railroads and was a director on the board of the Buffalo, Rochester, and Pittsburgh Railroad. His comments on this subject carried considerable weight with his colleagues.

Miner belabored Bartholomew and Associates with a few of his own pet projects. He wrote an especially vivid memorandum about a traffic problem at Chestnut and Gibbs streets where they intersected with East Avenue, a location that his office in the RG&E Building overlooked. The completed report was widely distributed to the public. The City Council officially approved the street plan submitted by Bartholomew; however, as the Depression deepened in the early 1930s, and city revenues plunged, most of its ambitious projects were put aside.

In June 1931 Miner was one of the speakers at another National Conference on City Planning held in Rochester. He acknowledged that, in earlier years, he had optimistically forecast the implementation of a number of projects in the city plan that had not come to pass. "When I discussed the city planning scheme with the local political authority of that day," Miner remarked, "he listened with as much detachment as if I were discussing the movement of the remoter nebulae in outer space. . . . We had to deodorize the 'City Beautiful' idea and call it by the more practical designation of the 'City Plan.'"

The implementation of large municipal projects in cities generally moves at a glacial pace, facing the challenges of achieving popular support and navigating through the required levels of approval. Ned Miner, at the age of seventy, no longer had the patience for his job on the board. He wrote the City Manager that the present setup of the City Planning Board was "a joke" and resigned from the board in 1934. Despite his frustrations, Ned's influence in planning his city's development over the previous twenty years was significant and was reflected in many improvements and new buildings, like the Genesee River beautification and the Civic Center, which came into being before and after he left the board, respectively.

As the new president of the Chamber of Commerce in 1909, Miner took the initiative in promoting support from Chamber members and the general public to create a United Charities organization to coordinate charitable giving among the dozens of charitable agencies and churches in Rochester. The Rochester General Hospital, of which Miner was a director, was one of the first enterprises to become a member of the new organization. Not every one signed on. Some other churches and organizations, like the YMCA, preferred to raise funds independently. United Charities later evolved into the Council of Social Agencies in 1923, which provided training and other services to its member organizations and worked closely with the Community Chest in the distribution of its funds.

The Community Chest of Rochester had started up in 1918, with George Eastman as president of its board and Ned Miner as a member of its executive committee. Eastman was the inventor, founder, and head of the Eastman Kodak Company, which produced photographic products, like the "Brownie" camera and film. Kodak products dominated the consumer market for years, and the highly successful company became the leading employer in Rochester. George Eastman was, for many years, the leader and city's most generous benefactor in funding civic, cultural, and educational institutions, including the University of Rochester.

Ned Miner was also a team captain in the Red Cross drive in 1918 headed by George Eastman, the Chairman of the Rochester Chapter. Through the 1920s he worked with Eastman in various causes, including the Rochester General Hospital and projects at the University. In 1929 Miner wrote Eastman:

Dear George;

Benjamin Franklin had a birthday once, something like you are having today, at which time his friend, George Washington, took occasion to write him a letter of congratulation, and this is what he said:

"If to be venerated for benevolence, if to be admired for talents, if to be beloved for philanthropy, if to be esteemed for patriotism, can gratify the human mind, you must have the pleasant consolation to know that you have not lived in vain."

Thinking the matter over, I am inclined to the view that George stated the matter conservatively, and that there is no reason why it cannot be passed on to you, with the added satisfaction that while the words are George's the sentiments are mine.

In 1931 Miner worked with Thomas J. Watson, head of IBM, in planning a large, formal Society of the Genesee dinner in honor of George Eastman at the Commodore Hotel in New York City, attended by leading businessmen and public officials. The following year, to the great sorrow of Ned Miner and all of Rochester and beyond, George Eastman, the city's leading citizen, took his own life. His departing message was, "My work is done. Why wait?"

Miner was an organizer and the first president of the Civic Music Association, which brought together all of Rochester's musical enterprises in 1930 and would later struggle to stay afloat during the Depression. He helped develop the Rochester Public Library, the Reynolds Library, the Rochester Museum of Arts and Sciences, and the Rochester Historical Society. He was a trustee of the Rochester Community Chest, the Rochester General Hospital, and the Family Welfare Society. He was a member of the City Planning Board, and on Sundays carried out his vestryman's duties at St. Paul's Church. Ned Miner put in a full workweek.

Rochesterians treated E. G. Miner with great respect—from the doorman at the Genesee Valley Club to the CEO of Eastman Kodak. There were many Rochester causes and projects that benefited from Ned Miner's shrewd judgment and generosity, and in his senior years his fellow citizens chose to honor him formally. In 1940 Miner was awarded the Rochester Civic Medal at the annual gathering of the Rochester Museums Council, a black-tie dinner attended by five hundred Rochesterians who applauded loudly when Mayor Samuel B. Dicker presented the silver medal to him.

President Alan Valentine of the University of Rochester gave the opening citation:

The true annals of man's progress will recount first of all its quiet stewardship by men like you. Captains and kings may flourish and depart, but often leave behind them only aimless tracks across the path of progress. Your part has been more modest, and more effective. Accepting the men and materials at hand, choosing to make your service here and now, rather than dramatically in remote places; you have advanced human ideals and institutions close at home. For your successful devotion to that more helpful task we do you honor.

The record is long and clear. The program of this Convocation lists but a few of the media through which you have worked for public welfare and private culture. The list is long and impressive, but less so than the years of daily self-giving that lie behind it. The record is clear, but not so clear as your devotion to the development of the arts, the sciences, and of public humanity among your fellow-citizens. In nearly all of Rochester's cultural gains for forty years you have been a leader.

But the written record is not enough. Always generous in material things, your greatest gifts have been of another kind—the constant benefaction of your time, your wisdom, your energy, and your humor.

The owner of the richest chuckle in Rochester, that chuckle is not the least of your contributions to the health and happiness of its citizens. Behind the constant aroma of your cigar, and your profound inspection of its lengthening ash, your fellow-workers know from experience, lies a constantly active mind, at once practical yet imaginative, at once shrewd yet idealistic. Behind that cigar lies a quizzical eye, and within that eye a twinkle. How many times in the last fifty years have you not brought unity among men, just at the most difficult moment, by the sly interpolation of some apposite story—a story all the more effective for its slightly saline flavor . . . ?

I count it a privilege to embarrass you with this citation. For this privilege, as for many others, I am largely indebted to you. But for you I should not be in Rochester, among whose chief cultural pleasures I count my association with you. I present you, then, to receive this Civic Medal, as a token of the high and grateful regard of your fellow citizens.

In 1944 the Rochester Chapter of the Sons of the American Revolution awarded its Good Citizenship Medal to Edward G. Miner at a large public dinner at the Chamber of Commerce. Miner had served as the first secretary of the Rochester Chapter of the Sons of the American Revolution, his own membership deriving from Clement Miner, his great-great grandfather, who had been a second lieutenant in a Connecticut militia regiment during the Revolutionary War. The tribute to Miner was given by Arthur C. Parker of the Rochester Museum, who stated, "Born in Waverly, Morgan County, Illinois, in a year when there was a war between the states, you have ably emulated another great Illinoisan whose law office was not too far away from your boyhood home. In your character are the same iron and the gold that made Lincoln tower over the great among mankind. You, too, have the same sense of humor and a deep understanding of human nature."

In citing Miner's services to the city, Parker noted his gifts of rare books and historic materials to the University Library, the Rochester Museum, the Rochester Public Library, and the Rochester Historical Society, to which he also gave some of his own writings on local history. Said Parker,

You are the most sought-for president among us, and you have served many institutions, clubs, industrial corporations, and banks. . . . Who among us could be a vestryman of the Church of St. Paul, a member of The Club, the Fortnightly Club, the University Club, Country Club, and the Genesee Valley Club, and still keep a level head and democratic poise, of the Monroe County Republican variety? Who among us, indeed, could

advise or head a great corporation like the Pfaudler Company and its sub-
sidiary branches and still find time to read the classics, write authoritative papers for scholarly societies, and then sit in council with a railroad
company to keep its finances on the track? Who else could think of the
needs of a university library and the academic values of a highly partic-
ular university, while at the same time directing our Chamber of Commerce, which you served as president? No one ever did all these things
save Edward Griffith Miner. . . .

The America of now needs good citizens like you. For many years you
have demonstrated what a good citizen should be, for it is by their works
that we know them. . . . Good and great nations are built and sustained by
good citizens, and by them alone; and with you, our medal citizen, we shall
have a living example for our emulation.

In 1945 the Rotary Club conferred on Edward G. Miner its Rotary Civic
Achievement Award for the year. The award was given to the Rochesterian who
"through his life and work has contributed in a very significant manner to those
interests and activities that tend to make this city a better placed to live." The
presentation took place at a luncheon meeting in the ballroom at the Powers
Hotel, where, according to the press report, Miner was "flanked at the speak-
er's table by a near score of the city's religious, civic, educational, business, and
industrial leaders, most of them his personal friends. . . . His wife and a circle of
her close friends occupied a front table during the presentation ceremonies."
Ned Miner accepted all of these awards with characteristic modesty, remarking
to a friend, "You can't sit around a town for seventy years and not have a certain
amount of honor fall on you."

VII. The Miners of Argyle Street

Helen Miner was married to her prominent and outgoing husband for fifty-five years until Ned died in 1955. Friendly and old-school proper, practical, petite, and modest, she chose to stay quietly in the background of her husband's busy public life, which was the conventional role for most women in her time. As she grew older, her style of dress seemed quite old-fashioned, certainly to her grandchildren—lace-collared, dark dresses with a black hat perched on top of her coiffured white hair. She adored her grandchildren, visited their families to see them, and wrote them often. The last letter her grandson Tommy Lamont wrote home from his U.S. Navy submarine in the Pacific in March 1945 was to his grandmother Miner. His submarine and all its crew were lost a month later.

Helen, who had attended Miss Porter's School in Farmington, Connecticut, worked hard at raising money on the boards of her favorite charities, including the Women's Educational and Industrial Union and the Strong Memorial Hospital, where, for many years, she was on a women's committee that oversaw the School of Nursing. To plan their fundraising programs, the ladies often gathered at elegant tea parties, which Helen rode to in the family's little electric car. Its maximum speed was fifteen miles an hour, which, Ned Miner declared, "was fast enough for Helen."

Ned Miner, "with the richest chuckle in Rochester," was a very congenial fellow—good company, everyone agreed. Mercer Brugler, president of the Pfaudler Company after Miner, said he was "an excellent companion. His conversation and wit enlivened all those occasions when friends and business associates gathered for social or business reasons." He was wise, he was erudite, and he was amusing. A fellow University of Rochester trustee described him as a "jovial companion," and a Rochester newspaper columnist reported, "He is an excellent raconteur and delights in good food and lively fellowship." He also liked good Bourbon whiskey, fine wines, and cigars. A prize collector's item in Ned's vintage wine cellar was a case of 1815 Prince of Wales port wine.

Ned joined a number of clubs—the Genesee Valley Club, the Country Club, the Pundit Club, The Club, the Century, and the Fortnightly Club—and enjoyed the camaraderie of their functions, often men's dinners. He also was a nonresident member of clubs in a few cities that he visited frequently, such as the Union League Club and India House in New York and the Saturn Club in Buffalo. Miner was the only noncollegiate member of the University Club, although he received honorary degrees from Hobart College and the University of Rochester. His library and clubs were his favorite recreational activities, rather than the golf course, a game he played infrequently with mediocre results.

When the Miner children, Elinor and Ranlet, were in their late teens, the family chose to spend summer vacations on the island of North Haven in Penobscot Bay, Maine. While they had tried the Adirondacks and other spots in previous years, the low-key, informal atmosphere of the North Haven summer community appealed to them. During the school year, Elinor, whom her father called "Sister," attended Miss Porter's School at Farmington, Connecticut, and Ranny was a student at St. Mark's school in Southborough, Massachusetts, where his father wrote him the following letter:

Dear Sonny,

When one gentleman makes another gentleman a present of most of the second hand ties that he has, it is incumbent upon the second gentleman to make a fitting acknowledgement; that is the reason I am inquiring whether you received them.

Just the same, these were good ties, and if you don't like them, send them back, for they will still be in fashion at No. 2 Argyle Street. . . . Since you are not close enough to enable me to help you to turkey on Thanksgiving, I am sending you in lieu of that our love and good wishes and the hope that the day will be pleasantly happy for you.

It was in North Haven that the Miners' pretty and vivacious daughter Elinor, known as Ellie, met and fell in love with Thomas S. Lamont. Tommy Lamont was the oldest son of Thomas W. Lamont, whose family had a summer house in North Haven. T. W. Lamont was a prominent Wall Street banker, a key partner in the firm of J. P. Morgan & Co., where Tommy would soon start to work. The Miners rented a house on a grassy knoll in the village where the young folks got together at the small yacht club for sailing races and picnics.

In 1922 E. G. Miner wrote a handwritten letter to T. W. Lamont:

My dear Lamont:

Your son has come today asking me to give him my daughter, and he has gone away happy with her and my blessing. . . . When that time comes for your Eleanor [Lamont's daughter] I hope that you may have the equal comfort and satisfaction that I feel in giving my Elinor to Tommy. Elinor has shown me your good letter to her and I am glad that you and I agree in our appreciation of our children.

The local society editor reported on the marriage in 1923 of Elinor B. Miner and Thomas S. Lamont in typical fashion: "Society has long awaited the Lamont-Miner wedding, and fashionable St. Paul's Church was filled to the doors yesterday with one of the most select groups that has gathered for any single function this year." Edward G. Miner in his formal black cutaway proudly led his daughter down the aisle and gave her away. Elinor's gown of cream satin was trimmed with lace that her mother had worn at her wedding. After their honeymoon the Lamonts would live in New York City, where Tommy was working at J. P. Morgan & Co.

Edward G. Miner and his daughter's father-in-law, Thomas W. Lamont, hit it off well. In 1929, when Miner was a trustee of the University of Rochester, the University awarded the honorary degree of Doctor of Laws to Lamont at their June commencement exercises. Lamont had been a key member of the U.S. delegation in Paris that year to resolve the question of German reparations under the Young Plan. The two corresponded, discussed business conditions with each other, and sometimes Lamont offered Miner investment advice on promising stocks.

In 1930 the Miners' son, Ranlet, married Anne Lindsay from Rochester in another elegant wedding ceremony at St. Paul's Church. Ranlet joined the Pfaudler Company and would become very helpful on company matters to his father, who was about to become chairman of the board.

I remember my grandfather, Ned Miner, when he was older—portly, with white hair parted right down the middle. He was kindly and courtly in his manners; his nails were manicured, and he was always meticulously dressed. He was hardly ever without a jacket, vest, and tie, and often wore a dark, double-breasted suit, his tie adorned with a pearl stickpin. I remember his special panache in carving the turkey at Christmas dinner and in smoking his cigar in the library, surrounded by his beloved books. I was fascinated by the suspenseful lengthening of his cigar ash. How long would it hold up?

John Macomber, a grand nephew who lived near the Miner home, reported that his Uncle Ned was always generous with kindly, wise, and practical advice. "One of his memorable quotes that has stayed with me was, 'Always give a dollar's worth of work for fifty cents' worth of pay,'" delivered, said Macomber, when his work habits clearly needed improvement. "More often than not, our sessions came to a close with a newly minted silver dollar pressed in my hand, a lot more special than a paper dollar bill."

My Miner grandparents came from Rochester to New York City to attend my graduation from Buckley School in 1941 and traveled to Exeter, New Hampshire, to attend the graduation of their oldest grandson, Tommy Lamont, from Phillips Exeter Academy in 1942. Tommy gave the senior class oration at the commencement exercises. His grandfather Miner wrote him the following letter on his eighteenth birthday a few months later:

You were my first grandchild, and your birth meant a great deal to all of us. I was in the Milwaukee Club, Milwaukee, Wisconsin, when the telegram came telling of your arrival, I was sitting talking with Governor Frank L. Lowden, and he suggested that we have a small bottle of champagne and drink a toast to the young man, which we did. . . . Time has gone so fast since that day that I have not realized that all of a sudden, my grandson had grown to man's estate. . . . I have loved you all through the years, as only a grandfather can, and I tried to tell you this in my awkward way when I saw you last at Exeter.

Your Class oration that day made me proud beyond words. . . . I know that you will make your life worth while and that all of us will be proud of your work. Whatever you do, wherever you go, you will always carry with you the love and hopes and prayers of us all.

You will have your periods of doubt as to the future; you will have your disappointments that men will not rise to the best that is in them, and are content to live among the husks and swine. But if you keep your faith in ultimate truth, decency and goodness, you will come out in the end strengthened for the conflict, which runs through a man's experience.

Be true to yourself, and at the same time have infinite charity for your fellow man who does not see the light, as God gives you to see it. Be honest and charitable with those men who hold mistaken views, and scorn deceit as you would the plague; a man who is honest with himself and has charity in his heart for his fellow man will never lack friends. You will have disappointments, sorrow, doubts of yourself, and some suspicion of your fellow man at times—all the miseries which every man of honor has had since the beginning of history, but you can overcome these. A smile, a kind word, a gracious deed, no matter how small it seems to you, bulks large with others. Be charitable, and forgiving—it does not pay to hate. In other words, be a man, and God go with you.

The letter is reminiscent of Abraham Lincoln—"With malice toward none; with charity for all"—and Ned Miner's message of wise advice to his grandson well summed up his own principles for living a good and useful life. When I became engaged to Camille Buzby in 1950, grandfather Miner, at the age of eighty-seven, wrote me the following letter:

Grandmother Miner has your letter at home, telling of how the young lady has stolen your heart. . . . I gathered enough from her reading to me, that there is only one girl in the wide, wide world, and that you have persuaded her that Lamont is the best of family names. Please tell your bride-to-be that I send both Camille and yourself my warmest love and good wishes, and say, also, that I hope soon to have the pleasure of saying this in person to you both.

Good luck to you, my boy, and tell your lady love that you both have my warmest love and blessing.

Throughout his life, Ned also maintained close ties with his family back in Winchester. He wrote to his father, James, often, and paid for improvements to the old family home where his parents lived after his grandfather's death in 1900. Ned himself became owner of the house when James Miner, who outlived Ned's mother, Eleanor, died. Three of Ned's siblings then lived there for a number of years.

When Ned's daughter, Elinor Lamont, was expecting her first baby in 1924, her grandfather, James Miner, wrote her the following letter only a year before he died:

Dear Elinor,
Feb. 19, 1924

Your letter brought me the best piece of news I have heard for a long, long time. I am proud of you. Proud of the happy, joyful way in which you are looking at the condition of things. Proud of you because you are not ashamed to tell your old Grandfather all about it. When you were a little girl and used to visit here, I watched you playing around the place and often wondered what your future might be. I wish I had a dozen granddaughters, if they proved to be like you—and I should have a dozen or more, if my children had followed the example set them by their parents in the way of having children. Your grandmother and I had seven. Rearing children is lots of trouble and a big expense—but then they are the source of a great deal of happiness and pleasure. They are the ties that help to make a happy household. . . .

You ask me, "How I would feel if I became a Great Grandfather?" I'll tell you I would feel like Simeon of old, when he first caught sight of the infant Jesus and said, "Lord! Lettest now thy servant depart in peace, for mine eyes have seen thy salvation."

Good bye and good luck. As ever yours,
Jas. Miner

In 1954 Camille and I brought our infant son, whom we called Ned, to Rochester, where Helen and Ned Miner met their first great grandchild, Edward Miner Lamont Jr., and witnessed his christening at St. Paul's Church. The following year, on October 10, 1955, Edward G. Miner died, following a fall in his home that fractured his hip.

Bishop Dudley S. Stark and Reverend George L. Cadigan officiated at E. G. Miner's funeral service at St. Paul's Church, where a large crowd came to pay their last respects to a much admired and honored citizen of their city. Slowed down but active until the end, Ned Miner had attended a Pfaudler board meeting ten days before he died.

Mercer Brugler, president of the Pfaudler Company, said of Miner's death, "Mr. Miner was a man of the highest character, a loyal friend, and a business-man, who possessed an unusually high degree of vision, and an exceptionally alert mind. All of us in Pfaudler Co., both here and abroad, who have worked with him, loved, and respected him all these years. Mr. Miner had spent seventy-two active years with the Pfaudler Co., a record of service which few businessmen have the distinction of reaching. To me and to many others in our company he has always been a splendid example, a wise counselor, and a constant source of stimulation to our thinking and to our energies."

The Rochester Gas & Electric Corporation board, of which Miner had been a member for forty-five years and chairman for fourteen years, passed a resolution which listed his positions and said that they reflected "a well merited recognition of his competence and of his value as a wise builder and counselor in the field of civic, industrial, and cultural development. Throughout all the years he possessed a rare faculty of being able to evaluate the proper balance between humanitarianism and practicability in industrial relationships." The board expressed its profound sorrow at the passing of Edward G. Miner, "whose genial personality and wise, constructive counsel will be missed by all who have been privileged to serve with him."

University of Rochester President Cornelis W. de Kiewiet said, "As a member of the board of trustees for over forty years, its secretary for fifteen years and chairman from 1938 to 1945, his shrewd judgment, human optimism, and good sense played a large part in the planning and decisions that led the university from a small college to an institution of international reputation."

During the first half of the twentieth century, the city of Rochester experienced robust growth. Its population in 1900 more than doubled to 332,000 by 1950, accompanied by a large increase in the surrounding metro area, of which Rochester was the hub. A driving force was the growth of technologically advanced industrial companies led by the Eastman Kodak Company. During those years Rochester became a Mecca for successful startups of a number of prominent companies whose names became well known. Bausch & Lomb, the maker of optical equipment, became a flourishing Rochester enterprise, and its leader, Edward Bausch, was a generous patron of good works in Rochester. Haloid, the manufacturer of photocopying equipment (and predecessor of Xerox), was also a very successful Rochester company. Other makers of specialized products included Taylor Instruments, Stromberg Carlson, and the Pfaudler Company. The city's successful industrial and business expansion went hand in hand with the development of Rochester's civic, cultural, and educational institutions, which were generously backed by the leading corporations and their executives. The University of Rochester grew steadily in size and stature, and in the twenty-first century is the city's leading employer. Edward G. Miner was a vital force in contributing to his city's well being and progress during those fifty years of Rochester's vibrant growth.

The *Democrat and Chronicle*, a leading Rochester newspaper, wrote the following obituary after Miner's death:

Elsewhere in this newspaper will be found a list of the activities and honors of Edward G. Miner. . . . Too bad there can not be printed with them a transcript of his kindnesses toward others. . . . But those who benefited, even from some small show of thoughtfulness, will remember.

Rochester and the business world have lost a great industrial leader. The city has lost a great man. It is in that latter designation that he will be held longest in memory.

Achievement marked his life. Business success came to him early. He guided a young business into world importance. Then he retired from his presidency more than twenty years ago, only to find that there was always a demand for his keen mentality and for his restless energy.

Outstanding was his long service on the University of Rochester Board of Trustees, eight years as chairman. And the fact that he, no college graduate, was honored with a degree is evidence enough of the whole-hearted way in which he worked and served.

When the University of Rochester awarded the degree to Miner a decade earlier, President Alan Valentine in his presentation summed up Edward G. Miner's life story well: "You brought with you out of the plains of Illinois a little of Lincoln, much of Mark Twain, and just a suspicion of Paul Bunyan, and staid Rochester has profited from all three."

Acknowledgments

I am very grateful to all the folks who helped me gather material for this book. First, within my own family: My cousin Ranlet Miner provided a scrapbook kept by our grandmother containing newspaper clippings covering Ned Miner's career, as well as photographs and family papers describing events going back several generations. John Macomber, my second cousin, provided some delightful reminiscences of his Great Uncle Ned and observations on the Rochester business scene during Miner's life. My wife, Camille, known to everyone as "Buz," was helpful in many ways—providing computer technical assistance, preparing pictures for the book, and offering general encouragement and support. She accompanied me on all our field trips to Stonington, Winchester, Springfield, and Rochester, where she sorted and recorded all the materials that I needed to copy from the Miner papers housed in the University of Rochester Library.

In Stonington, my daughter, Camille, was our guide to the site of the old Minor farm and the Wequetequock Cemetery, where we viewed Thomas Minor's gravestone and the memorial shaft honoring him. At the Stonington Historical Society Library, Anne Thatcher Tate, the library director, and Frederick Burdick, president of the Thomas Minor Society, provided us with material on the Miner families in Stonington in the seventeenth and eighteenth centuries. In Winchester we talked with Richard E. Mann, a local attorney and historian, who directed us to the old Miner farm home. Dennis F. Suttles, genealogy research librarian at the Abraham Lincoln Presidential Library in Springfield, read my manuscript and provided useful advice. In Rochester, Julia Sollenberger, director of the Edward G. Miner Library at the University of Rochester School of Medicine and Dentistry, welcomed us and guided our tour of the library. I owe a special debt of gratitude to Nancy Martin, university archivist and Rochester collections librarian at the University of Rochester Library. She efficiently supplied all the papers from the Edward G. Miner collection that I had requested, and arranged the copying of selected materials. In addition, Nancy and her colleague Karl Kabelac read my manuscript and made a number of helpful editorial suggestions. I am also grateful to Suzanne E. Guiod, editorial director, and Ryan M. Peterson, managing editor, of the University of Rochester Press, for their guidance in organizing the production of my book.

Sources

Chapter I

The Diary of Thomas Minor (New London, CT: Press of the Day Publishing Company, 1899) is an important source for most of this chapter. It covers the years 1653 (when Minor first settled in Stonington) to 1784.

"The Minor Farm," by Craig Miner, in *Historic Footnotes: Bulletin of the Stonington Historical Society* (February 1975), is a useful summary of the diary.

"A Concise Stonington Chronology," in *Historic Footnotes* (February 1999), and drawn from Williams Haynes's *Stonington Chronology, 1649-1949: Being a Year-by-Year Record of the American Way of Life in a Connecticut Town* (Stonington, CT: Pequot Press, 1949), identifies key events during the seventeenth and eighteenth centuries.

Thomas Minor, Descendants, 1608–1981 (Trevett, ME: printed by author, 1981), by John A. Miner, provides an authoritative identification of the ancestry of Edward Griffith Miner (1863–1955), generation by generation, going back to Thomas Minor (1608–1690).

Miner and Allied Families of Connecticut and Long Island (New Haven: Donald Lines Jacobus, 1928), by Lillian Lounsberry Selleck, provides information on Thomas Minor from his birth.

"The Minor Family" from Ancestry.com and "Thomas Minor" from Genealogy.com summarize the life of Thomas Minor and his son Joseph based on various sources.

"Thomas Minor Family History" from Familyhistory.com, edited by Peter Miner, records the English origins of the Miner/Minor family as well as the life of Thomas Minor.

Charles Miner (Wilkes-Barre, PA: 1916), by Charles F. Richardson and Elizabeth M. Richardson, also summarizes the lives of Thomas and Joseph Miner.

"John Winthrop, Jr." (April 1999), an article from the Connecticut State Library, History and Genealogy Unit, gives a brief history of Winthrop's life, including his governorship of Connecticut in the 1600s.

History of the Town of Stonington, County of New London, Connecticut (New London, CT: Press of the Day Publishing Company, 1900), by Richard Anson Wheeler, provides town history and genealogical information on the Miners.

Mayflower (New York: Viking, 2006), by Nathaniel Philbrick, provides information on King Philip's War.

The above sources provided the information for the story of the Miners in Stonington during the seventeenth and eighteenth centuries. Books of general history were useful in providing the background of the times.

Chapter II

Memoranda and letters by E. G. Miner held by family. The E. G. Miner Papers held in the Department of Rare Books and Collections in the University of Rochester Library. There are 271 boxes of papers and a seventy-five-page catalog identifying the subject matter contained in each box.

"Diary of Trip to Illinois," by E. G. Miner, 1832.

"Winchester—Its Growth," "Primitive Conditions," and "Prominent Dead of the Community" from *Winchester Centennial Souvenir*, March 25, 1930, describe the town and events during 1800s.

"Life Sketches and Reminiscences of the Late E. G. Miner of Winchester," printed in the *Winchester Times* of January 22, 1909, is a brief biography of Miner.

Obituary of Mrs. E. G. Miner, *Winchester Standard*, April 3, 1891.

"Historical Memoranda Concerning Morgan and Scott Counties, Illinois," by James H. Riggs, *White Hall Register-Republican*, August 24, 1923.

Collected Works of Abraham Lincoln, vol. 2, The Illinois State Historical Library, Springfield, reproduces the letter from Lincoln to E. G. Miner. The Miner family holds the original letter.

Chapter III

Memoranda and letters by E. G. Miner, held by the family. The E. G. Miner Papers, held in the Department of Rare Books and Collections at the University of Rochester Library.

"Abraham Lincoln at Winchester 1854, 1858," by E. G. Miner, published in the *Winchester Times* in 1885.

"Abraham Lincoln, Personal Reminiscences of the Martyr-Emancipator," by Dr. James Miner, is an account of Lincoln's speech in Winchester in 1854, privately printed and later published in the *Winchester Times* of May, 25, 1923.

Winchester Times of May 25, 1923, also contains a reprint of an unidentified observer's account of Lincoln's speech, "Mr. Lincoln in Winchester" (originally dated 1858). There was no local newspaper in the Winchester area until the *Winchester Times* was established in 1865.

Winchester Centennial Souvenir, March 25, 1930, contains "The Lincoln Rally," by Judge John Moses, an account of Lincoln's visit and speech in Winchester in 1858.

The Lincoln Newsletter (Winter 1993) contains "Lincoln Speaks Out on the Kansas-Nebraska Act," by Dennis E. Suttles. (Largely based on James Miner's account, which is apparently the only original source for Lincoln's 1854 speech in Winchester.)

Letter of November 2, 1895, from E. G. Miner to his grandson E. G. Miner II in Rochester about his meeting with Lincoln on his 1858 visit to Winchester contained in E. G. Miner Papers.

"The Kansas-Nebraska Act and the Rise of the Republican Party, 1854–1856," by R. D. Monroe, Abraham Lincoln Historic Digitization Project, http://lincoln.lib.niu.edu/biography6text.html.

Abraham Lincoln (New York: Henry Holt, 1917), by Lord Charnwood.

With Malice toward None—The Life of Abraham Lincoln (New York: Harper and Rowe, 1978), by Stephen B. Oates.

The E. G. Miner Papers at the University of Rochester also contain an envelope enclosing two pieces of black ribbon which the label identifies as coming from Lincoln's catafalque at the State House in Springfield, when Lincoln's remains lay in state there in 1865.

Chapter IV

Memoranda and letters by E. G. Miner, held by the family. The E. G. Miner Papers, held in the Department of Rare Books and Collection at the University of Rochester Library.

Standard Atlas of Scott County, Illinois, 1903 (Chicago: George A. Ogle & Co., 1903) contains a brief biography of Dr. James Miner.

"James Miner of Winchester," by Carl E. Black, MD, reprinted from *Illinois Medical Journal* (May 1928), is a biography of Dr. James Miner.

Civil War service of Dr. James Miner, including his meeting with General Ulysses S. Grant and his capture by Confederate soldiers at Holly Springs is taken from Miner's own account contained in E. G. Miner Papers.

"The One Hundred First Illinois," from the *Jacksonville Daily Journal,* Jacksonville, Illinois, May 30, 1909, describes the history of this regiment during the Civil War.

The American Heritage Picture History of the Civil War (New York: American Heritage, 1960).

"Raid on Holly Springs, Mississippi," This Day in History, December 20, 1862, http://www.history.com/this-day-in-history/raid-on-holly-springs-mississippi.

Personal Memoirs of U. S. Grant (New York: Dover, 1995), by Ulysses Simpson Grant.

Chapters V, VI, and VII

Memoranda and letters by E. G. Miner, held by the family. The E. G. Miner Papers, held in the Department of Rare Books and Collections at the University of Rochester Library.

An album of more than a hundred items, mainly newspaper clippings, covering Miner's life and career in Rochester from 1900 until 1955, collected and kept by his wife, Helen Miner.

"If You Live Long Enough," by William C. Bryant, a short biographical sketch of E. G. Miner in manuscript form, provides an account of Miner's participation in city planning for the city of Rochester held in the E.G. Miner Papers.

"Edward G. Miner," by John R. Russell, *The University of Rochester Library Bulletin* (Autumn 1955), describes Miner's participation in planning the building and development of the university library, and his contributions of rare books to the library.

"E. G. Miner to head Trustee Board," *Rochester Alumni Review* (1938).

University of Rochester News Release, December 17, 1952, announcing that the library of the School of Medicine and Dentistry would be named the Edward G. Miner Library.

Makers of Rochester, Brief Biographies of Prominent Citizens of Rochester, Bulletin of Rochester Museum of Arts and Sciences (Rochester: Rochester Museum Press, 1940).

Text of the address of Dr. Arthur C. Parker at the Sons of the American Revolution dinner honoring E. G. Miner, October 7, 1944.

Prospectus of the Pfaudler Company, preferred stock issue, May 10, 1902.

Pfaudler Reporter, Edward Griffith Miner Memorial Issue, October 10, 1955.

"History, Pfaudler Company," compiled by the Robbins Myers Process Solutions Group, http://www.pfaudler.com/history.php.

"Mr. Miner," Award of 1940 Civic Medal, presentation by Dr. Alan Valentine, the Pfaudler Company (1940).

"Resolution of Board of Directors of Rochester Gas and Electric Corporation," October 12, 1955.

Rochester: The Quest for Quality, 1890–1925 (Cambridge, MA: Harvard University Press, 1956), by Blake McKelvey.

Rochester: An Emerging Metropolis, 1925–1961 (Rochester: Christopher Press, 1961), by Blake McKelvey. (The two books by McKelvey provide a detailed history of the city of Rochester during the time of E. G. Miner.)